The Manual That Didn't Come With Your Computer (But Should Have) version.

written by Edward A McWhirter Jr

Acknowledgements
Thanks to Muriel Handwork for the idea to write the book.

Thanks to Barbara Barber, Muriel Handwork and Leslie McWhirter for content ideas for the book.

Thanks to Muriel Handwork, Kevin Dyer, Jim Vandermeer, Leslie McWhirter, Tara Sharp and Richard Tondreau for editing and more ideas.

The Manual That Didn't Come With Your Computer (But Should Have) version.

| 1

Table of Contents

Introduction

If things are designed perfectly it becomes unnecessary to write instructions for them because their intended use will be obvious. This isn't usually the case, so it is nice to have a manual to reference when something unfamiliar comes up. That's where this book comes in! I don't expect you to read it cover to cover; if you do, you may find that some subjects are repeated. Read it any way the is comfortable with you; if I had my way every copy of this book would have extra writing and dog ears on the pages.

I want this to be a way to help people find what they're looking for quickly or remember things they don't use all the time. It is possible, and very likely, that parts of this book will become dated, especially with how fast technology develops these days. Hopefully, this is because things are improving and becoming easier. I encourage you to make notes and changes as needed.

While I was writing this, I looked around for other books on the same topic. Most of the ones I found were either outdated or too complex for real beginners with computers. Some of them are in my references at the end of the book because I read them and got ideas for what to focus on and what to leave out. Even as I finish this writing, many things here are outdated or becoming outdated, but I hope it will still be useful as a reference for understanding and to give you a better idea of where to look for more information. Sometimes just knowing the terminology is enough to search for more information **online**.

Regular and frequent computer users probably know most of the things written here without even thinking about them, but not everyone has been told how all of it works, or they aren't sure where to look to find the information. I've also noticed that some people just don't want to or can't learn "this computer stuff." For this reason, I want to make a manual where you can just look up what you need. **Google** is an amazing search tool, but it doesn't help if you're not sure what you're looking for. Not yet anyway.

I try not to make many assumptions about prior knowledge so that anyone can find what they're looking for here, but it's impossible to feign naivety for long. That being said there are a lot of very simple concepts, and some complex ones, contained within. Some things are spelled out with where to go and what buttons to press with a certain task in mind. I hope that the concepts that are complex have enough explanation surrounding them to help you understand what you need to do without scaring you off.

If you're reading this, chances are pretty high that you are using a Windows **Operating System**, and almost as good that you're using **Internet Explorer**. If not stated explicitly, these are two assumptions I make. I also assume that your computer is in proper working order.

About This Book

As you read, you'll notice places with arrows (->) and plus signs (+). These are used to describe **keyboard accelerators**, or sequences of actions. Keyboard accelerators are **shortcuts** that help you avoid using the **mouse**. An accelerator or set of buttons with an arrow listed between two keys or buttons means that they should be pressed in sequence, one after the other. The plus sign indicates that they should be pressed at the same time.

Example: *"Shift + Enter"* indicates that you should hold the *Shift* key while you press *Enter*, and *Alt -> P* indicates that you should press and release the *Alt* key and then press the *P* key.

There is a very comprehensive vocabulary section at the back of the book. The first time a technical word appears on a page, it will be bolded to indicate that it is defined in the vocabulary section.

Chapter 1 – Computer Concepts and Vocabulary

The first thing I want to do is clear up some concepts addressed in this book that novice computer users frequently find confusing. There is a vocabulary section at the back of the book, so if there is a word relating to computers that you are unfamiliar with, try looking it up there. I've **bolded** all of the words that are in the vocabulary section the first time they appear on a page.

It is also important to note that things in the computer world can change fairly rapidly. **Programs** will change, go out of use, and new ones will be made. The notes in this book are accurate at the time of writing, but that doesn't mean they will be for long. The information here will still aid you in figuring out what you need, as well as being a nice useful computer reference.

Computer vs. Operating System (OS)

Your computer is the physical box that sits in front of or beside you. It is the piece of equipment you turn on when you want to do something. Desktop computers have nicknames like: "the tower" or "the box". This is what your **keyboard**, **mouse** and **monitor** are connected to. If you use a laptop, this still applies; everything is just much more compact and more tightly connected.

The **operating system** is what you interact with on your computer almost 100% of the time. This is what you see after your computer is finished **booting** when you press the power button. The operating system is what tells your computer how it is supposed to work. Some examples of common operating systems include **Windows XP**, **Windows Vista**, **Windows 7**, **Mac OS**, **Red Hat**, and **Ubuntu**.

The **Windows** operating systems, written by **Microsoft**, are almost always referred to as just "Windows" unless it is necessary to differentiate them. If you bought a **PC** that already had an operating system on it, it was probably a version of Windows. Some of the different versions of Windows include: **Windows 2000**, Windows XP, Windows Vista and Windows 7. Every couple of years Microsoft comes up with newer and better features and functionality for an operating system, so they bundle it up and sell it as a package. As of this writing, their most recent operating system is Windows 7, Windows Vista was short lived before that, and Windows XP was the long running popular operating system before that. Microsoft provides support for these operating systems when they come out, but eventually stop supporting the older ones.

The Mac OS only comes on **Apple** products like the **Mac Book**. Red Hat and Ubuntu are examples of **Linux** operating systems, which are normally distributed for free or with a fee for support. There are some corporations and businesses that use these **operating systems** for their power and flexibility.

If there is ever a significantly different way to do things on different operating systems, they will be listed under a heading with the title of the operating system. All operating system have the same basic functions and many sections in this book have operating system specific subheadings.

Computer vs. Hard Drive

The computer is the entire system; also referred to as the "tower" or the "box." All of your input and output **devices** like the **mouse**, **keyboard** and **monitor** are connected to the computer. Everything your computer needs to function is contained inside of it. You shouldn't ever have to access these things on the inside, but we'll talk about some of the things in there and what they do in other Chapters.

Your **hard drive** is the physical piece of equipment where all of your data is stored. Most hard drives use some sort of magnetic tape or disk to keep your data stored when your computer is turned off. This is one reason it is important not to store strong magnets near your computer. The hard drive is located inside of your computer. It is possible to connect other **external hard drives** for extra storage space, but there must be at least one internal hard drive.

The hard drive is also where your operating system is stored. When your computer **boots** up, it reads the operating system on the hard drive and loads it up for you. It's where all of your **documents**, music and other **files** are stored when you save, copy or **download** them. When your computer is on, the hard drive is usually called the "C" drive in your computer settings. There are **folders** and files on the C drive that help organize your operating system, program files, and other documents.

Internet vs. Internet Browser

The **Internet** is the large system of interconnected computers that allows people to store and look up information as well as communicate with people around the world. The Internet **Browser**, normally just referred to as "Browser," is what we typically use in order to connect to this wealth of information, but it isn't the only way.

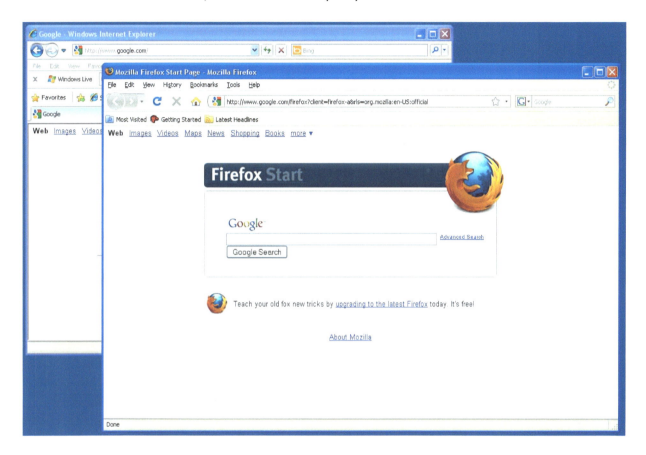

Browsers are used to look at websites, which are stored on the World Wide Web (www). Many people and businesses have websites these days. Your local bank and grocery store will almost certainly have a website so that you can get **online** to find out more about them. Websites can also have news, weather, recipes or anything else you can imagine, but you need to use a browser to get to them.

Some examples of common browsers are Mozilla **FireFox** , **Google Chrome** , **Internet Explorer** , **Opera** and **Safari** . Most computers you will come into contact with will come with a type of Browser. You can also find and **download** different browsers for free; there are websites just for the purpose of downloading **software**. Internet Explorer comes standard on Windows machines, and Safari comes standard on Macs.

E-mail, or **electronic mail**, is just another small portion of all the things that can be accessed on the Internet. There are so many different kinds of e-mail that are available like Gmail ,

Yahoo Mail 📧, Hotmail 📧, and AIM/AOL Mail 📧. You can tell which mail provider people use by the part of the **e-mail** address after the '@' symbol. For example, if my e-mail address were computer.help.book@gmail.com (which it is), you could tell that I use Gmail to send and receive e-mails. Some providers even offer the option to forward e-mail from another provider so that you can have multiple accounts but still look in one place for all of your e-mail.

Homepage vs. Browser

Your **homepage** can refer to a couple of different things. When you open a **browser**, the first webpage that it shows is your homepage. This webpage is typically located on the **Internet**, and the browser retrieves it when opened, or a copy is stored (**cached**) on your computer.

Some examples of browsers are **Firefox** 🦊, Google Chrome 🌐, **Internet Explorer** 🧭, **Opera** 🅾️, and **Safari** 🧭. Your homepage within any of these browsers can be any web page on the Internet or stored on your computer. It can even be different for each browser.

Mac vs. PC

Technically, PC is just short for 'Personal Computer.' Your PC is the computer you use at home to surf the web, play games, and write reports. The reason for the confusion is that PC is also the term that is used to refer to most computers that are running Windows.

A **Mac** is just another name for a PC that was created by the company **Apple**. They create **hardware** and **software** and sell it as a bundle to you. Macs have their own **operating system** called the **Mac OS**. Just like versions of Windows that upgrade and change, the Mac OS iterates through versions of the operating system. At the time of this writing, they are on Mac OS X, nicknamed Snow Leopard.

Finding Information About Your Computer

If you are calling or e-mailing someone for computer help, it could help to know a little information about your computer. There are a couple of ways to do this, but this is the easiest.

Windows XP – computer properties

Right-click on your "My Computer" **icon** on the **desktop** or in the **start menu**, then click on "Properties". The window that comes up has some of the essential information about your system listed.

1.1 - Windows XP System Properties. Open by right-clicking on the "My Computer" icon and selecting "Properties."

Starting at the top there is a heading that says "System" which lists the things relating to your **operating system**. It includes the version of Windows you're running as well as the **Service Pack** that has been installed and some other version information. This computer is running Windows XP Home Edition updated to Service Pack 3.

Next is listed who the computer is "Registered to" followed by "Computer" which contains **hardware** information. The hardware list includes the type of **processor** your computer has followed by the amount of **memory** (**RAM**) it has. This computer has an Intel Core 2 Duo processor that runs at 2.66GHz, and has 3.25 **GB** of memory.

Hard Drive Space

Your **hard drive** is where all of your **files** and **programs** are stored. When your computer is turned off the hard drive continues to store all of your information. Your computer will tell you when you run out of space; you won't be able to save any new items. Any time you save a file it is being saved to your hard drive.

If the **hard drive** starts to run low on space, one easy way to get more is to delete old **files** that you don't want and don't use anymore. If you don't want to delete anything, you can also copy your old files over to **writable CD**s, **Flash drives**, or **External Hard drives**. Once they're copied over to the other media, you can delete them from your computer. I recommend leaving files that you didn't create alone. Your **operating system** and other **programs** create files that they need and use, which means that it is impossible to clean your hard drive up completely. If you don't know what a file does, leave it alone.

For comparison, a CD normally holds about 700MB of information. There are 1,024 **MB** in a **GB**. If you have a small hard drive (40GB or less) you will probably need to clean up your hard drive fairly often. If you have a large hard drive (200 GB or more) you probably won't need to clean your hard drive up nearly as much unless you save lots of larger files. To put this in perspective a recordable CD can hold about 150 songs or 500 pictures worth of data, but can't hold a single full length movie.

Another way to clean up space is to remove programs that you have installed that you don't want or need anymore. This is described in chapter 10. You can also use the **Disk Defragmenter** mentioned in chapter 10 to aid you in freeing up some hard drive space.

Windows XP – disk defragmenter

Double-click "My Computer" then right-click on your C: drive and go to "Properties."

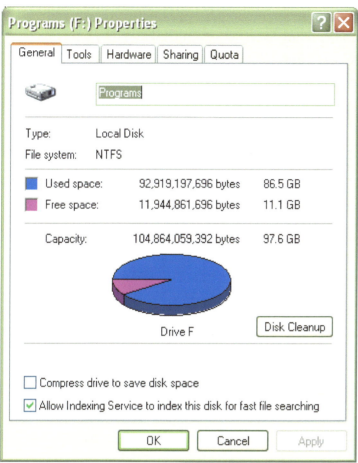

1.2 - Windows XP Hard Drive Properties. Open by right-clicking on your listed hard drive (C:) and selecting "Properties."

This shows you the total size of your hard drive as well as how much space you have used in a handy little pie chart. The pink slice shows how much hard drive space is free. The number of bytes listed isn't really important since it converts the number to **Gigabytes** for you on the right.

Windows Vista

Go to "Computer" -> "Control Panel" -> "System and Maintenance" -> "System." This contains most of the information about your computer. It starts with the "Windows edition" heading which contains the version of Windows and the **Service Pack** you're running, such as Windows Vista Home Premium and Service Pack 1. Next, is the "System" heading which contains **hardware** information such as **processor** and **memory**.

Linux: Ubuntu

In the menu bar click "System" -> "Administration" -> "System Monitor" then go to the "System" tab. This will list the version and build you're running, followed by how much memory and what kind of **processor** you have and how much space your **hard drive** has.

Maximize/Minimize/Restore/Close Programs

These are the group of three buttons that appear at the top right of most **programs**. They only apply to Windows and **Linux** operating systems. The '*minimize*' and '*close*' buttons are always in the same place, but the '*maximize*' and '*restore*' buttons take turns. If your program is not already *maximized*, the *maximize* button shows. If it is *maximized*, the *restore* button shows. The *maximize*, *minimize* and *restore* buttons look like a very miniature version of your screen and are supposed to show you what will happened to the screen if you press them.

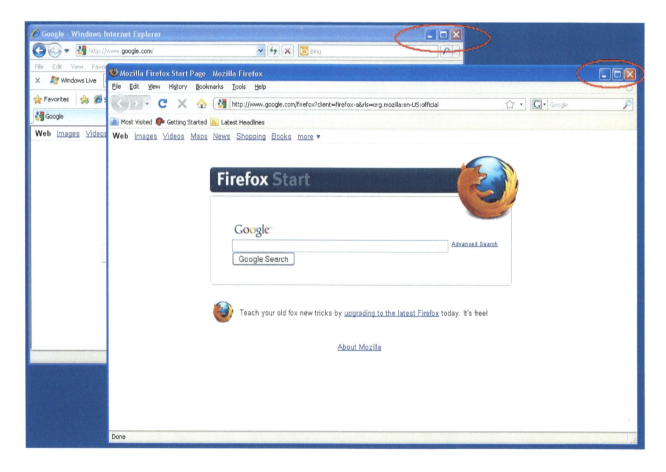

Maximize

The *maximize* button is a rectangle with a thick top line, also called the "title bar." The line at the top looks similar to the menu bar at the top of most **programs**. This button only shows up if the program is not already *maximized* and it is allowed to be. Some windows won't allow you to *maximize* them. You can also double-click on the **title bar** to maximize if it isn't already.

Figure 1.3 - a) Microsoft Word "Restored" on the screen in Windows XP. This is basically "unmaximizing" it.

This button makes your program or window expand to fill up the whole screen as shown below. You can't move the program around on the screen if it is *maximized*, but you can still *minimize*, *restore* or *close* it.

1.4 - Pressing the "maximize" button makes the program fill the screen.

Minimize

The *minimize* button is located at the top left of most **files**, programs and windows and it has a short line at the bottom of it. This is supposed to be reminiscent of the taskbar, which is a line of text boxes at the bottom of the screen.

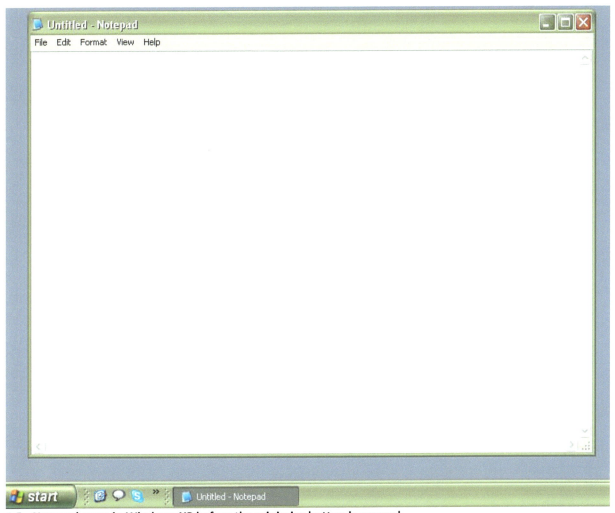

1.5 - Notepad open in Windows XP before the minimize button is pressed.

The **minimize** button makes your **program** or window 'hide' down in the taskbar. In the taskbar it shows up as a rectangle with an **icon** on the left for the program and a few words that summarize where you were at or what you were working on. In the figure above, there is a rectangle in the taskbar that represents the text **file** that is open in **Notepad**. It is titled as "Untitled – Notepad" because I haven't given it a name, but this tells you that the name of the file is "Untitled" and it is open in the "Notepad" program. When the minimize button is pressed, the **Desktop** looks like the figure below.

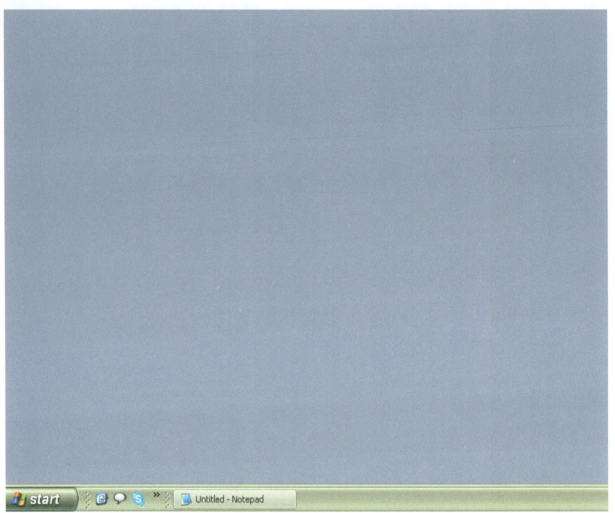

Figure 1.6 - Notepad open in Windows XP after the minimize button is pressed. It is now only showing down in the taskbar.

Figure 1.7 - Section of Taskbar showing a text file open in Kate in Red Hat Linux after the minimize button is pressed.

There is a **shortcut** in Windows XP to minimize all Windows: Windows Key + M

Restore

In Windows this button looks like two windows overlapping each other, in other **operating systems** it sometimes just looks like a very small rectangle within the button. It only shows up if your **program** is *maximized*. You can also double-click on a maximized window to restore it.

Figure 1.8 - a) Microsoft Word "maximized" to fill the screen. b) Pressing the "restore" button shrinks it back down and allows you to move it around the screen.

The *restore* button brings windows or **programs** back to the dimensions they were before you maximized them. When your program is restored it is possible to move and overlap programs and windows with each other.

There is a **shortcut** in Windows XP to restore all Windows: Windows Key + Shift + M

Close Programs and Documents

The *close* button is the easiest of these. It appears as an 'X' at the top right of your program. Clicking on this closes the program or other window that the 'X' belongs to, such as a **file** within a program, or the program itself.

Right-click Taskbar -> "Close"

If the "X" doesn't work, or if the program is **minimized**, you can right-click on the program down on the taskbar. Then select "X Close."

Alt + F4 (Windows and Linux)

If you're going to use this one, make sure the program you want to close is either the only one open, or you're sure it is on top of everything else that is open. Otherwise you may end up closing something you didn't intend to. Just hold Alt and press F4 once.

Windows XP

Task Manager (Ctrl + Alt + Del)

If things aren't responding and don't seem to be moving (a **program** is **frozen**), you can force programs to close by using the task manager. Just hold Alt + Ctrl and press Delete. In the "Applications" tab you can select a program then hit the "End Task" button at the bottom. A box that states the program is not responding will come up, at which time you'll click "End Now."

Folders/Directories/Files

Folders, or directories as they are sometimes called, are what your computer uses to stay organized. Folders can hold any number of **files**, and folders can be contained within folders within folders and so on. This is just like your home filing system, but with fewer size limitations regarding your folders.

Creating a New Folder

Folders are a great way to organize your files into common groups. For example, you can create a folder on your **desktop** called 'Pictures2009.' Then inside of that folder you can store some pictures from 2009, and even create a couple more folders called 'Halloween' and 'Christmas' for storing some of your holiday pictures.

Windows XP

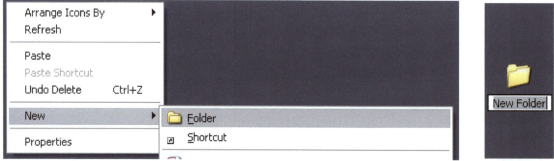

Figure 1.7 - a) Create a new folder in Windows XP by right-clicking on the desktop and going to New -> Folder. b) The new folder will appear with the name highlighted so you can change it.

Right-click on any blank spot on your desktop or inside of another folder, then go to 'New' -> 'Folder'. A new folder will appear in the location you clicked with the name of 'New Folder' highlighted so that you can change it.

Linux: Ubuntu

Right-click on any blank spot on your desktop or inside of another folder, then select "Create Folder." A new folder will appear in the location you clicked with the name highlighted so that you can change it.

Linux: Red Hat

Right-click on any blank spot on your **desktop** on inside of another **folder**, then select "Create New" -> "Folder…"

Figure 1.8 - In Red Hat Linux a box is displayed for naming a folder when you right-click on the desktop or in another folder and choose "Create New" -> "Folder…"

Type a name for the folder in the box that comes up and press "OK."

Rename Folders

Select the folder and press F2.
or
Right-click on the folder in question -> "Rename."
or
Click twice slowly on the folder (slower than a double-click).

Zipped Folders

Zip **files** are handy for compressing big files or groups of files so that they can be sent to someone else, or stored somewhere. Creating a zip file is the act of grouping and compressing the file or files, and opening a zip file is the act of uncompressing it so that you can look at the files.

Creating a Zipped Folder

Begin by creating a new folder as mentioned above (Folders/Directories/Files -> "Creating a New Folder" section). Then move or copy the file(s) you want to compress into the new folder.

Windows XP

Next right-click on the folder -> Send To -> Compressed (zipped) Folder.

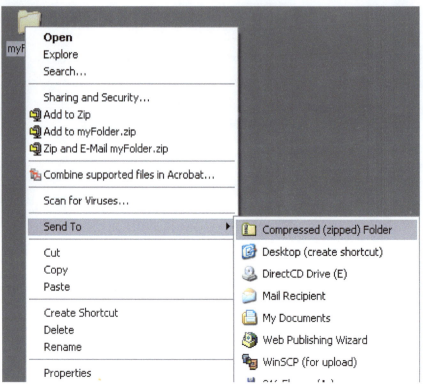

Figure 1.9 - To create a zipped file in Windows XP, right-click on the folder and go to Send To -> Compressed (zipped) Folder.

This will create a zip **file** with the name of the **folder** as shown below.

Figure 1.10 - The zipped file will look like this with the same name as the folder it was created from.

You may get a message box like this one:

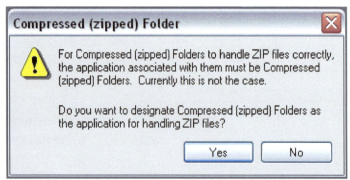

Figure 1.11 - This message may come up when you zip a file in Windows XP. Your answer really doesn't matter.

If you're going to compress files in this way all the time, you can choose "Yes," if not you can choose "No." Either way, your zip file will be created.

Opening a Zipped Folder

Windows XP

Right-click on the zip **file** and choose the "Extract to folder C:\..." option. The file path that it shows will just be the path where the file is currently at. If you're on the **desktop**, it will create an extracted **folder** on the desktop.

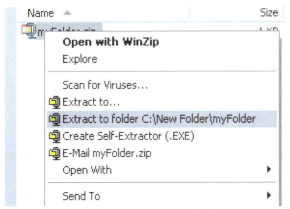

Figure 1.12 - In Windows XP, right-clicking on a zip file brings up options that allow you to extract the file so that it can be read.

The folder name will be the same as the zip file was excluding the ".zip" part.

Chapter 2 – Shortcuts and Keyboard Help

These will save us some time and confusion later. Shortcuts help you move around your computer and accomplish tasks more quickly and efficiently. Shortcuts can refer to **icons** on your **desktop** that open **programs** or **documents**, or they can refer to key combinations that help make tasks easier and faster.

Conventions: In This Book and Elsewhere

Instead of writing out something like:
    Hold the SHIFT key as you press the letter G on the **keyboard**.

The following syntax with the plus sign (+) to say the same thing:
    SHIFT + G

The key or keys listed before the plus sign(s) should be held down while the final key is pressed to get the desired effect.

For a sequence of events, an arrow (->) will be used to specify order. For example instead of saying:
    Go to the menu bar, click "File," then click "Save."

We will write:
    File -> Save

Whenever you are clicking buttons up in the file menu of a program, and the option ends with an ellipsis (...), that means that a box with more options will be brought up if you click it. This is the easiest way of telling you that there is an opportunity to cancel your action(s) if it isn't what you want.

Keyboard

Not all keyboards are exactly the same, but most are close enough to find the correct key. There are only slight differences in location.

Ctrl/Alt/Shift

There are three keys on your **keyboard** that are used for changing the effects of the other keys on the keyboard. They are the Control, Shift and Alternate keys. These three modifier keys are always used by holding them down, then pressing the key you want modified. For example holding the SHIFT key then pressing the letter 'C' will give you a capital letter C on the screen; assuming you have selected an area that accepts text. Holding the CTRL key and pressing the letter 'C' will copy any text you have selected to the **clipboard** (discussed in chapter 4).

On the keyboard they can be labeled in different ways:

    Ctrl = CTRL = Control Key
    Alt = ALT = Alternate Key
    Shift = SHIFT

The CTRL and ALT keys are almost always abbreviated in this way because they aren't used as often so they are smaller keys. The SHIFT key is larger because it is used quite often for making capital letters and using the symbols above the number keys. All of these are on the keyboard in two places to aid in using both hands easier.

Tab

The Tab key can be used to move through blanks in paperwork and other forms on your computer and **online**. The Tab key will almost always take you to the next field in the form.

Alt + Tab

To cycle through **programs** that you have open, just hold the Alt key and press Tab repeatedly until the program you wish to be on top is highlighted then let go of Alt. While the Alt key is held down in this manner, you can see all programs you currently have running on your computer.

Alt + Shift + Tab

While you're using Alt + Tab to cycle through open programs, you can hold the Shift key in addition to the Alt key you're already holding. When you press Tab with both of these down, you will cycle backwards through the list of programs instead of forward.

Tab

Tab is used quite a bit when filling out forms online, or for cycling through fields in a program. When the cursor is in a field, you can press the Tab key to move to the next field.

Shift + Tab

You can move backwards through forms just as easily as going forward with Tab by holding the Shift key and pressing the Tab key.

Enter

Inside of any kind of word processor, this just creates a new line. In a form where you enter values in blanks, this is normally equivalent to hitting "Next" or "OK" or "Finish."

Backspace/Delete

Backspace and delete are both for removing unwanted characters. If you're on a Windows machine, the biggest difference is that backspace removes the character that is immediately in front of the cursor, while delete removes the character immediately following the cursor.

If you're on a **Mac**, the delete key is the one that removes characters immediately in front of the cursor, and there is no backspace key.

On the **keyboard** they can be labeled different ways:
Del = DEL = Delete
Backspace

Delete can also be used for deleting **files** by selecting them and pressing delete. Backspace doesn't work for this.

Caps Lock

This acts as though you are holding the Shift key, but for letters only. If you need to type several things using capital letters, this will help prevent your pinky from getting tired holding down the Shift key.

Num Lock (Number Lock)

The **Num Lock** key is located at the top left of the Numpad on most keyboards. The Numpad is the small rectangular set of keys normally separated from the other keys slightly and almost always on the right side of the keyboard.

The Num Lock key turns the Numpad on or off. When the Num Lock is on, the numbers on the keys can be used. When Num Lock is off the other functions on the keys can be used (like the arrows).

For example, if you're working in **Word**, when the Numlock is turned on and you press the number '7', you will get a 7 in the text area. When the Numlock is turn off you will be taken to the beginning of the line the cursor is on (Home).

Function Keys

The Function keys are located along the top of the **keyboard**. There will be commands throughout the book that use the Function Keys for shortcuts. They are labeled as F1, F2, F3, etc.

Some examples of uses for the Function Keys.
F1 – Typically brings up the help **file** for the selected **program**.
F2 – Can be used to rename selected files or **folders** while they're highlighted.
Alt + F4 – Closes the current program, file or window.
F5 – Often used to bring up the 'Find' tool for searching for particular text.
F6 – Take the cursor to the **address bar** in most **browsers**.

End

Within a webpage in a browser, this will take you to the bottom of the page. In text editors it will take you to the end of the line the cursor is on.

Home

Within a webpage in a browser, this will take you to the top of the page. In text editors it will take you to the beginning of the line the cursor is on.

Creating and Using Files/Documents

With so many different ways to make or look at files, it can be confusing and cumbersome. If you know what you want to do, but aren't sure where to start, this will get you on track and give you a basic idea of what things are used for. I recommend browsing through your start menu to see what kinds of **software** you have available on your computer.

Letters/Reports/Text Files/Papers/Word Documents

This is one of the more common tasks that most people need to accomplish on their computer; writing a letter, taking notes, writing papers, etc. There are several programs that were designed with this in mind.

Notepad also comes standard on most Windows machines, and contains no formatting. It is only capable of opening, saving, printing and changing font style and size. **KEdit** on some **Linux** machines is the approximate equivalent of Notepad.

Notepad can typically be found by going to Start -> Programs -> Accessories. (Windows only)

WordPad is a very simple **document** editor with very minimal formatting options. It comes standard on most Windows machines, and is capable of changing fonts, using bold, italics, underline, and center or left justify. It can also print documents, but that is about the extent of its abilities. **KWrite** has similar functionality as WordPad for a **Linux** machine. **Kate** is also available on some Linux machines and has all of the same functionality plus some other tools.

WordPad can typically be found by going to Start -> Programs -> Accessories. (Windows only)
KWrite can typically be found by going to KMenu -> Utilities -> Editors. (Linux only)

Microsoft Office Word, referred to in short as **Word**. **Word** is a very comprehensive word processor that normally comes as part of **Microsoft Office**. It can do everything WordPad can, plus much more. It is a **formatter** as well as a **word processor** and editor. Word allows you to insert objects like pictures, **clip art** and charts into your documents, as well as create simple tables.

Microsoft Office Word can typically be found in the **start menu** under Programs -> Microsoft Office

OpenOffice Writer is similar to Word in many ways. It even allows you to insert pictures and export documents in **PDF** format. It is installed with **OpenOffice**, which can be **downloaded** for free from:
    http://www.openoffice.org/

Spreadsheets/Lists

Spreadsheets are useful for making tables of information that are more complicated than what you can do in a word document. They are capable of storing equations that will calculate numbers based on what you put in other places on the spreadsheet. For example you can create a row of numbers that represent how much money you spend on groceries in a month, then at the bottom you can have a cell that sums the entire row for you automatically.

These are great for organizing finances, or other data you wish to look at, especially since they can be turned into charts and graphs that are easier on your eyes.

Microsoft Office Excel , referred to in short as **Excel**. It normally comes with Microsoft Office. It has a very large selection of equations and charts, as well as much of the same formatting that is available in word processors.

Microsoft Office **Excel** can typically be found in the **start menu** under Programs -> Microsoft Office

OpenOffice Calc is similar to Excel in many ways. It is installed with **OpenOffice**, which can be **downloaded** for free from:
    http://www.openoffice.org/

Pictures/Images

Pictures are everywhere and it's nice to be able to look at them, organize them, and sometimes even change them.

Paint comes standard on most Windows machines. It can open and save most picture **file** types (.gif, .bmp, .jpg, .png), as well as do some simple picture edits involving text and simple colors and shapes.

Paint can typically be found by going to Start -> Programs -> Accessories. (Windows only)

Picasa Photo Viewer is made by **Google**, and is free to download. It works similar to Windows Picture and Fax Viewer except that you can also use it to manage your pictures **online**, and you can open a picture in another program on your machine from it.

Picture Manager often comes with copies of **Microsoft Office**. It has some slightly more powerful tools than paint, including cropping and resizing.

Windows Picture and Fax Viewer comes standard on most Windows machines. It's not much good for editing images, but it can rotate, zoom in on, and print them. **KView** is a **Linux** equivalent to the Picture and Fax Viewer for Windows.

QuickTime Picture Viewer comes with some versions of **QuickTime** (the media player). It is similar to Windows Picture and Fax Viewer in its abilities.

GIMP comes standard on some Linux machines. It can open, edit, and save most picture file types, as well as do some fairly complex picture edits.

Resize An Image

Paint

Image -> Stretch and Skew (Ctrl + W)
Change the percentages under "Stretch" to something besides 100% and the image will be made larger or smaller accordingly when you press OK.

Picture Manager

The [Edit Pictures...] button will bring up a side menu with editing options. Select Resize under "Change picture size." There are three different options for resizing. Choose the one that easiest for you then press "OK."

Slideshows/Presentations

Microsoft Office PowerPoint, referred to in short as **PowerPoint**. It normally comes with **Microsoft Office**. It is an easy to use tool for creating slideshows and presentations.

OpenOffice Impress is similar to **Excel** in many ways. It is installed with **OpenOffice**, which can be **downloaded** for free from:
    http://www.openoffice.org/

Selecting Objects in Lists or Documents

Drop Down Lists

Many forms have drop down lists for selecting values. Instead of scrolling through these lists with your **mouse**, you can use the letters and arrow keys on your **keyboard**.

Country: [–select country– ▼]

For example if I wanted to select 'United States' from a list of countries, I could hit 'U' which would take me down to 'Uganda.'

Country: [Uganda ▼]

Then I can use the down arrow or click the mouse on the right arrow to find 'United States.'

Country: [United States ▼]

Other Lists and Documents

Ctrl and Shift are very useful keys for selecting objects in lists, on website forms, or in **folders** on your **hard drive**. If it is possible to select more than 1 option in a form you can do so by selecting the first, then while holding Ctrl you can select any number of other options.

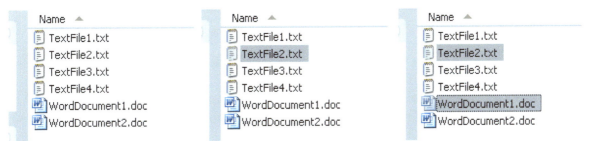

Figure 2.1 - a) Click somewhere in the folder. b) Click on one file in the folder. c) Hold CTRL and click on another file in the same folder.

If you want to select a range of objects you can click on the first then hold Shift and click on the last in order to choose the span of objects.

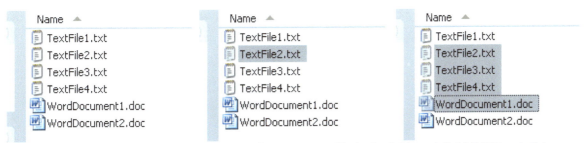

Figure 2.2 - a) Click somewhere in the folder. b) Click on one file in the folder. c) Hold SHIFT and click on another file in the same folder.

In folders on your hard drive you can also use Ctrl + A if you just want to select everything.

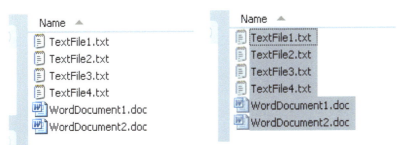

Figure 2.3 - a) Click somewhere in the folder. b) Hold CTRL and press 'A' to select everything in the folder.

If you are inside of a **document** window you can use Ctrl + A to select all of the text. Just click inside of the text area, then press Ctrl + A.

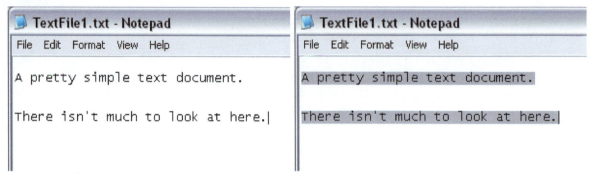

Figure 2.4 - a) Click somewhere inside the text file. b) Hold CTRL and press 'A' to select everything in the file.

When you're inside of a **folder**, it is also possible to select groups of **files** by "lassoing" them. Just click and hold the left **mouse** button down in any empty space within the folder, then drag the box around all of the files you want to select and let go of the mouse button.

This selection tool will be in the shape of a rectangle with corners at the points where you pressed and where you released the mouse button. If this method selects something you don't want, just hold CTRL and click on each item you want to deselect.

The same idea works for text in a **document**. Just hold down the left mouse button and drag the cursor over the text you want selected.

Font Size

Assuming you are looking at a **browser** window, you have these options. This is website specific.

Ctrl + '+'

To make the font size larger hold the CTRL key and press '+' (plus sign), which is most easily found to the right of the NumPad.

Ctrl + '-'

To make the font size smaller hold the CTRL key and press '-' (minus sign), which is most easily found at the top right of the NumPad.

Windows XP

This will change the font size for **title bars** and **icon** labels only.

Right-click on the **desktop** -> Properties -> Appearance tab. Under "Font size:" select "large fonts" and Click "OK."

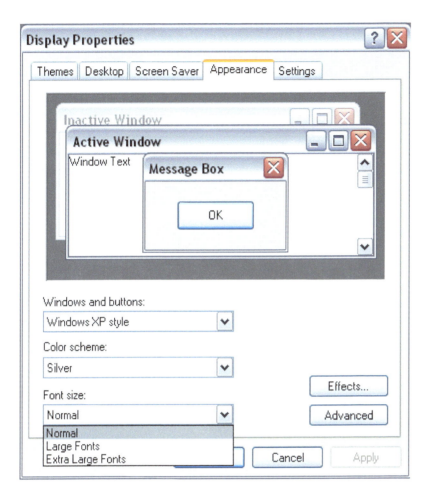

Figure 2.5 - In the desktop properties box for Windows XP, under the "Appearance" tab, there is a section for increasing the font size of Window labels.

If this is still too small, you can choose "Extra Large Fonts" instead.

Shortcut Icons

Most **icons** that show up on your Desktop are actually just **links** to the **executables** of other **programs**. These are typically referred to as **shortcuts**. With shortcuts you don't have to remember what **folders** to look in to find particular programs. There can also be icons for **files** on the Desktop, which typically look similar to or the same as the **application** they belong to. These are not shortcuts, because they are actual **documents**. The name of the document will be listed below these.

In this Desktop snapshot there are several icons on the desktop. The three at the top right (**Word** , **Excel** , and Mozilla **Firefox**) are all shortcuts, and are denoted by the small diagonal arrow in the lower left corner of the **icon**. Deleting **shortcuts** from your **desktop** does not delete the **program** they belong to. So if your desktop is getting cluttered it is safe to delete the ones you don't use. Just click on them once and press delete, or right-click on them and select delete. You can get them back by finding the program they belong to in the **start menu** and right clicking on its icon there. Then select Send To -> Desktop (create shortcut).

Figure 2.6 - a) Click on the desktop and hold the mouse button down. b) Drag the square lasso around the files you want to select and let go of the mouse button to select all items contained within the border drawn with the mouse.

The two icons at the top left (My Computer and My Documents) are Windows icons, and are **links** to your **hard drive**, or **folders** on your hard drive. Even though they don't have the arrow in the lower left corner, they are still technically shortcuts, and deleting them won't actually delete your hard drive, or your **documents** folder. The folder at the bottom right (New Folder) is an actual folder saved on the desktop. So deleting this will delete the folder and everything contained within it.

The three icons at the bottom left are documents (TextFile1.txt, Letter.doc, and MySpreadSheet.xlsx). These are actual documents stored on the desktop so deleting them will delete the document you had saved there. They can be deleted by clicking on them and pressing delete, or right-clicking and selecting delete.

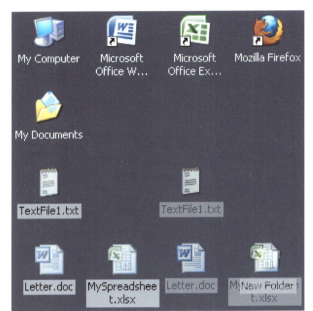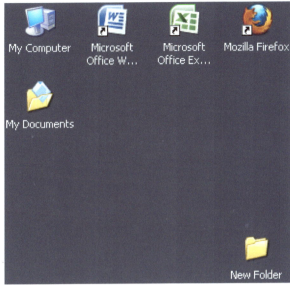

Figure 2.7 - a) Single click and hold the left mouse button on any one of the files you have selected (refer to figure 2.6). b) Drag the mouse pointer over the folder and release the mouse button to move the selected files into the folder.

These can be moved to a different **folder** by clicking on them and dragging them over the folder you want them saved in. For example I can select the Letter.doc, TextFile1.txt, and MySpreadsheet.xlsx and drag the **mouse** pointer over New Folder with the mouse button still held down, then release the mouse button over the folder, and the **documents** will be moved to the New Folder. You'll notice that while dragging the **icons** with the left mouse button held down, there will be a translucent copy of the icons following the mouse. This serves as a confirmation to show which documents you're going to move.

The actual **executable** files that these shortcuts **link** to are stored in folders on your **hard drive**. It is best not to modify these directly as it could cause them to no longer work.

Chapter 3 – Devices

There are so many **devices** that can be attached to your computers these days; all of them help you put information on, or take information off of your computer. Some of the more commonly used devices include **memory sticks**, **printers**, **digital cameras**, and webcams.

These devices typically come with **software** CDs, which aren't always necessary. Sometimes they contain **drivers** that you do need, but most often you can just plug your device in and it will work. If your device doesn't work how it is, then you should resort to installing any software that it came with. Digital cameras, **external hard drives**, memory sticks and **monitors** don't usually need any extra software installed to make them work, but printers normally do.

Device Plugs/Jacks

The back of a computer can be intimidating if you don't know what all of the connections are for. Most computers don't have exactly the same connectors in the back. We'll go through this one from top to bottom to give you a taste of what goes where.

At the very top is the power supply. The power cord runs from here to your outlet to give the computer power. Next are the two circular purple and green plugs. These are called PS2 ports, and they are for a **mouse** and **keyboard**, if your mouse and keyboard aren't **USB** style.

The next two rectangular orange ports are for external SATA hard drives. SATA is the name of the connection, which is newer and faster than IDE connections used inside the computer.

The next set of 6 round plugs are the audio jacks. The important ones to note here are that green is for **speakers**/headphones and pink if for a microphone.

The two black rectangular spots with the larger port with lights to the right of them are **USB** ports. Most **devices** are transitioning to USB ports. This can be anything from a **keyboard** and **mouse** to a webcam or **printer**. The port with the lights to the right is the Ethernet port. This is for an **internet** connection.

Monitor connections are next on the list. The one on the left is for one of the types of digital input for a monitor. It usually has a white end on the cord. The one on the right is for monitors with analog input, and it usually has a blue head on the cord. These two types of ports have holes for screws on the sides, and the cords have screws attached to them so that they can be held in place more firmly. They have lots of small pins inside, so the screw help keep things from jostling around so the pins don't break off.

Digital Cameras

Cameras don't need to store pictures and videos on film anymore. They can store it directly to digital media which can be copied directly to your computer. Many **digital cameras** have a USB cord that can be used to plug it directly into your computer. They can also have **software** that is supposed to help you move pictures from your camera, but this isn't necessary.

While the camera is plugged into your computer, and the power is on for both, the camera should show up as another **hard drive** under 'My Computer.' It will be listed somewhere below your 'C:' drive. If you navigate onto the camera and find the pictures, you can copy them where ever you want on your computer.

Memory Sticks

Memory sticks are small devices used for storing or backing up information as well as transferring **files**. Storage size for memory sticks these days is around 128Mb to 32 **Gb**.

Memory sticks can either be independent devices, normally with a USB plug on them, or they can be contained within another device. Digital cameras contain memory sticks, which is why most digital cameras come with a USB cord that can be used to connect the camera to your computer. Memory sticks are also sometimes referred to as thumb drives or **flash drives** when they have a USB hookup. While a memory stick or digital camera is plugged into your computer it will show up with your list of drives under 'My Computer.' From there you can access any files contained on the memory stick.

External Hard Drive

External hard drives work kind of like very large **memory sticks**, except that they also need to be plugged in. They will normally have a **USB** cord to plug into the computer as well as a power cord that needs to be plugged in to access the **hard drive**.

Printers

Adding a Printer

Windows XP

Step 1

The path to get to the printers can be slightly different depending on what kind of **start menu** you're using, and how the control panel is set up. If you're having trouble finding it, there are a couple of possibilities listed below.

Start -> Printers and Faxes -> Add a printer (upper left side, under "Printer Tasks")

or

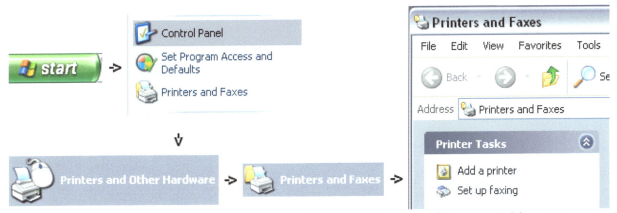

Start -> Control Panel -> Printers and Other Hardware -> Printers and Faxes -> Add a printer (upper left side, under "Printer Tasks")

or

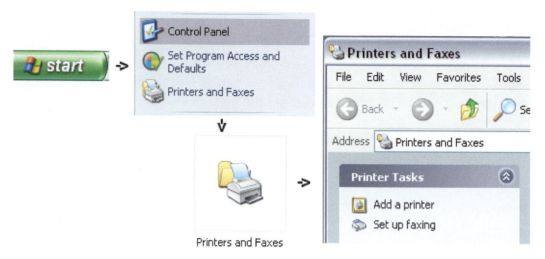

Printers and Faxes

Start -> Control Panel -> Printers and Faxes -> Add a printer (upper left side, under "Printer Tasks")

<u>Step 2</u>

Click "Next" then choose whether the **printer** is connected directly to your computer (Local) or it is somewhere on the **network** in your home or office (Attached to another computer or directly to the network; probably in another room). Then click "Next" to move on.

If it is a network printer you will either need to know the path of where it is located on the network, or you will have to browse for it.

Set a Printer as Default

This is how you choose which printer **documents** will go to without you having to select it every time you want to print. If you use Ctrl + P this is the printer it will go to automatically.

Windows XP

Start -> Printers and Faxes -> right-click on the printer you want, then click "Set as Default."

or

Start -> Control Panel -> Printers and Faxes -> right-click on the printer you want, then click "Set as Default."

Windows Vista

Go to Start -> Printers -> click on printer -> click on "set as default" button just under the **file** bar.

Sharing a Printer

This is an option that is available for a **printer** that is connected directly to your computer. If you want other computers on your **network** to be able to print to your printer, you just have to share it so they can find it. After you share it, other users just follow the steps for "Adding a Printer" above.

Windows XP

Go to Start -> Printers and Faxes -> right-click on the printer you want to share and go to Properties. Click the "Sharing" tab and select "Share this printer" then click "OK."

Printer Settings

One of the most common settings you may need to change between prints is whether the page is oriented vertically (**portrait**) or horizontally (**landscape**). Typically, switching between these settings won't change anything on the screen, only when you print. The default for most **programs** is portrait, so you'll probably only need to change this setting if the printable area isn't wide enough for your project.

Landscape Printing

Excel 2003

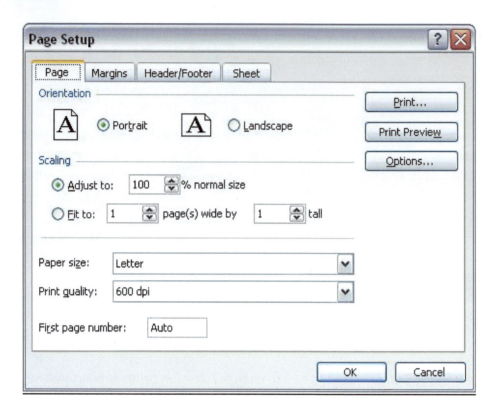

File -> Page Setup... -> Select "Landscape" under "Orientation" -> click "OK"

PowerPoint 2003

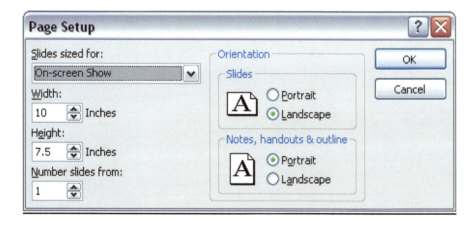

File -> Page Setup... -> Select "Landscape" under "Notes, handouts & outline" inside the "Orientation" section -> click "OK"

Word 2003

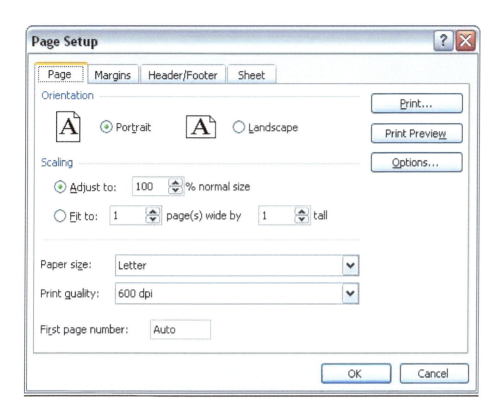

File -> Page Setup… -> Select "Landscape" under "Orientation" -> click "OK"

Excel 2007 , *Word 2007*

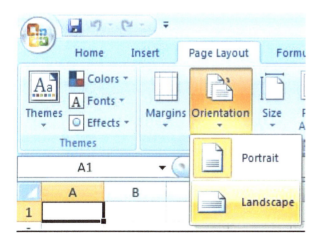

Page Layout -> Orientation -> Select "Landscape"

PowerPoint 2007

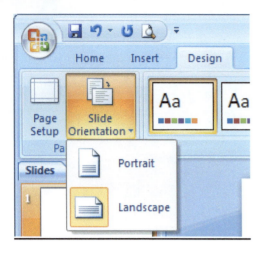

Design -> Slide Orientation -> Select "Landscape"

Firefox:

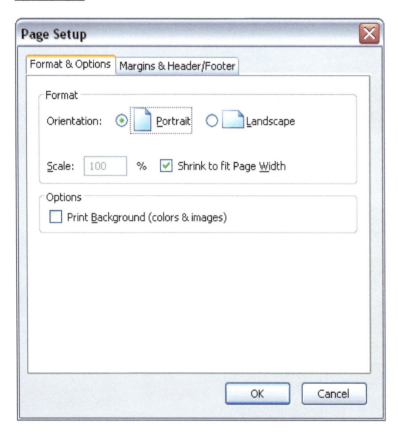

File -> Page Setup -> Select "Landscape" -> click "OK"

Internet Explorer: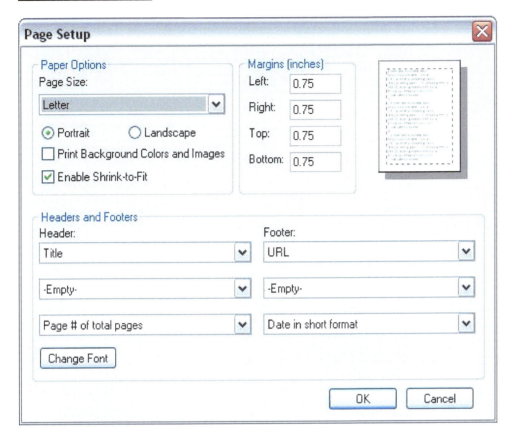

File -> Page Setup... -> Select "Landscape" under the "Paper Options" -> click "OK"

Opera: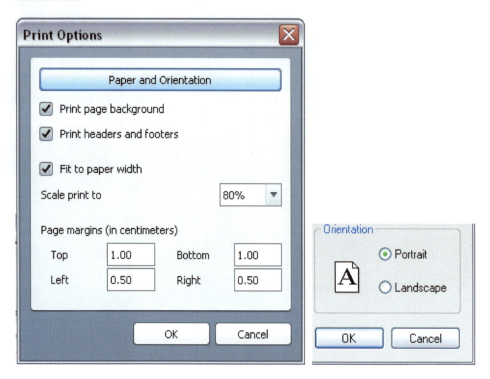

File -> Print Options -> Paper and Orientation -> Select "Landscape" under "Orientation" -> click "OK" -> click "OK" again

Safari: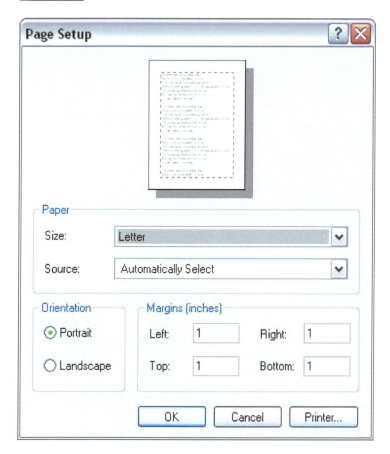

File -> Page Setup -> Select "Landscape" under "Orientation" -> click "OK"

Webcams

Webcams work almost exactly like video cameras except that they display the information directly to your computer immediately. These typically connect to the computer using **USB**, and they can be very useful for things like video conferencing over the **Internet**.

Chapter 4 – Copy, Cut, Paste and Other File Tasks

These three commands are often used because they can simplify your work on the computer when you understand them. They can be used inside of a **document**, or when looking at **files** in a **folder**. Typically you will cut or copy some text or files, then paste them somewhere else. These commands work uniformly on Windows and **Linux** systems.

Copy (Ctrl + C)

When you copy text or a file, you can think of it as being stored on a **clipboard** until you're ready to Paste it. On the simple clipboard, only one item can be copied or cut at a time, so you must paste before you copy or cut again if you don't want to lose your work. The original text or files you selected will remain intact. Hence a copy is made to your clipboard. You can copy text in a document, or copy a file or group of files.

Copy Text

Inside the document select the text you want to copy using the **mouse** or the cursor, then right-click on the highlighted portion of the text and click on "Copy." Equivalently, you can to press Ctrl + C after highlighting the text.

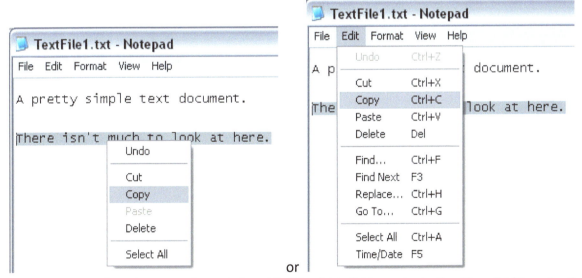

4.1 - Copy a line of text in Notepad on Windows XP a) by right-clicking and selecting "Copy." b) by using the Edit menu.

You can also use the "Edit" menu, which always contains the Cut, Copy and Paste commands, even though they are grayed out sometimes. They are grayed out when you aren't allowed to use them, or it doesn't make sense to use them. One reason they are normally grayed out is that you haven't selected anything.

Copy Files

Inside of the **folder** right-click on the **file** or group of files you want to copy and click on "Copy." Once again this is equivalent to pressing Ctrl + C. This can also be performed after selecting several files using one of the methods mentioned in the **Shortcuts** chapter (Chapter 2) under the **Selecting Objects in Lists or Documents** section.

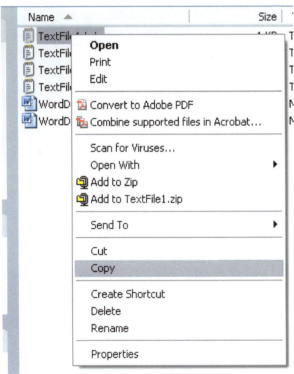

4.2 - Copy a single file in a Windows XP folder by right-clicking and selecting "Copy."

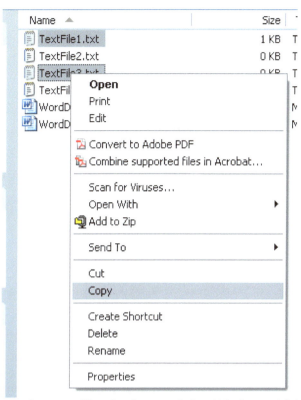

4.3 - Copy two files simultaneously in a Windows XP folder by selecting both files then right-clicking and choosing "Copy."

Cut (Ctrl + X)

Cut is similar to Copy, with one very important difference. Your original text or file is removed from its current location. It is still available on the **clipboard**, but you must paste it before you copy or cut again if you don't wish to lose it.

Cut Text

Inside the **document** select the text you want to remove or move somewhere else and press Ctrl + X or right-click and go to "Cut." You can also use the "Edit" menu, then go to "Cut."

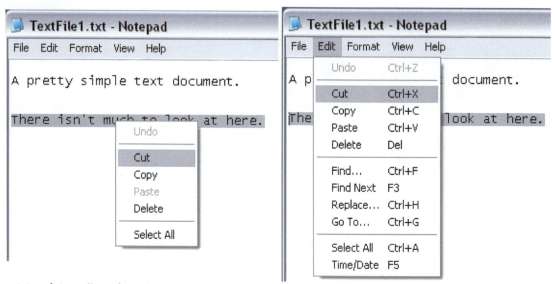

4.4 – a) Cut a line of text by right-clicking and selecting "Cut" in Notepad on Windows XP. b) Use the Edit menu to Cut text in Notepad on Windows XP.

Cut Files

Cutting **files** works the same as copying them except that they will be removed for the **folder** you cut them from.

Paste (Ctrl + V)

Paste is used to place things that have been copied or cut into another location. As long as you don't copy or cut anything else, you can paste the same thing as many times as you wish.

Paste Text

To paste something you have copied or cut, just place the cursor where you want the text to appear and press Ctrl + V or right-click and select "Paste."

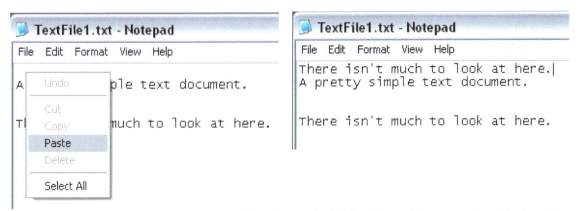

4.5 – a) Right-click on a location in the text (first line on the left in this case) in Notepad on Windows XP to paste a line of text that was previously copied or cut. b) After the text has been pasted it appears in the document where the cursor was located when the command was selected.

Paste Files

To paste **files** that you have copied or cut from another location, just click the **mouse** in the **folder** you want them placed in and press Ctrl + V or right-click and select "Paste."

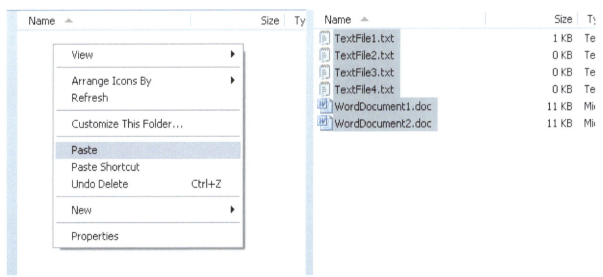

4.6 – a) Right-click in a folder on Windows XP and select "Paste." b) The files that were previously copied or cut from another location will appear in the folder.

Rename Files

Select the file and press F2.
or
Right-click on the file and select "Rename."

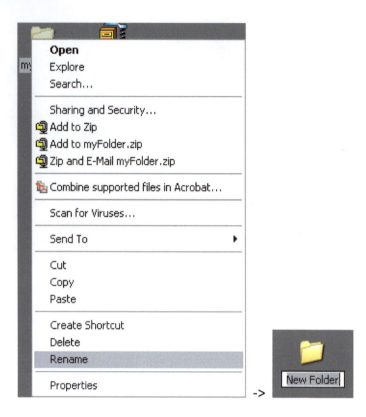

->

or

Click twice slowly (just slower than a double-click) on the **file** name in a **folder**.

Moving Files

The **mouse** is the easiest way to move files. Just click the mouse down on the file you want to move and drag it to the new location then let go of the mouse button.

Chapter 5 – Opening Files, Even Without the Correct Program Installed

If you don't have **Microsoft Office** (**Excel** [.xls, .xlsx], **PowerPoint** [.ppt, .pps, .pptx], **Word** [.doc, .docx], etc.) installed on your computer, it can be difficult to view **files** that are sent to you of this type. Don't worry though, there are a couple of ways around this and most of them are free.

OpenOffice

Using **OpenOffice** is one way to view, edit and save these files. You can **download** this **software** for free at http://download.openoffice.org/. It works for Excel (📊 **OpenOffice Calc**), PowerPoint (📊 OpenOffice Impress) and Word (📊 **OpenOffice Writer**) files among others. If you don't want OpenOffice, **Microsoft** makes free viewers for users to look at Microsoft Office files, but then you won't be able to make changes.

Microsoft Options

The Microsoft website is always changing so some of these **links** may not work, or may not be convenient to type in, but you can always search for them. I have provided the search keywords that I used in **Google** to find all of these downloads. You can also browse the Microsoft website, the starting point for downloads at the time of writing was: http://office.microsoft.com/en-us/downloads/
From here there is a list of download categories on the left-hand side.

If you have Microsoft Office 2003 and are trying to open files made in Microsoft Office 2007, you just need the Compatibility Pack:
http://www.microsoft.com/downloads/details.aspx?displaylang=en&FamilyID=941b3470-3ae9-4aee-8f43-c6bb74cd1466
Click the "Download" button -> "Save File"
Double-click on the "FileFormatConverters.exe" **executable** to begin the installation.

Google Search: Microsoft Office 2007 compatibility pack

Microsoft also has a page that lists all of their viewers here:

http://office.microsoft.com/en-us/downloads/HA010449811033.aspX

Excel

Excel Viewer

This can view any Excel **files** saved in the 2007 or earlier format. It replaces all other versions of the Excel Viewer/Reader.

1. **Download** the Excel Viewer at: http://www.microsoft.com/downloads/details.aspx?familyid=1CD6ACF9-CE06-4E1C-8DCF-F33F669DBC3A&displaylang=en
2. Click the "Download" button -> "Save File" (save it to a location you will remember, like "My Documents")
3. Double-click on the "ExcelViewer.exe" **executable** to begin the installation.

Google Search: Excel Viewer

PowerPoint

PowerPoint Viewer

This can view any PowerPoint files saved in the 2007 or earlier format. It replaces all other versions of the PowerPoint Viewer/Reader.

1. Download the PowerPoint Viewer at: http://www.microsoft.com/downloads/details.aspx?FamilyID=048DC840-14E1-467D-8DCA-19D2A8FD7485&displaylang=en
2. Click the "Download" button -> "Save File" (save it to a location you will remember, like "My Documents")
3. Double-click on the "PowerPointViewer.exe" executable to begin the installation.

Google Search: PowerPoint Viewer

Word

Word 2007 Reader

This can view any Word files saved in the 2007 or earlier format. It replaces all other versions of the Word Viewer/Reader.

1. **Download** the Word Viewer at:
   http://www.microsoft.com/downloads/details.aspx?FamilyID=3657CE88-7CFA-457A-9AEC-F4F827F20CAC&DisplayLang=en
2. Click the "Download" button -> "Save File" (save it to a location you will remember, like "My Documents")
3. Double-click on the "wordview_en-us.exe" **executable** to begin the installation.

Google Search: Word Viewer

PDFs

PDFs are a type of **file** that can be used by almost any **operating system**. They typically don't allow editing unless you have the correct **software**, like Adobe Acrobat professional.

Adobe Reader

1. Download Adobe Reader at (you can uncheck any boxes that are shown by "Also install"): http://get.adobe.com/reader/

2. Click on the "Download" button -> then you may have to "Allow" Adobe to **install** software on your computer, which is typically safe to do.

3. Click "Install Now".

Chapter 6 – Internet Browsers

There are several common **Internet Browsers**, which all have very similar features, but aren't always exactly the same. The ones I focus on are **Mozilla Firefox**, **Google Chrome**, **Internet Explorer**, **Opera**, and **Safari**. You only need to have one **browser** in order to surf the **Internet**, but you can also have all of them installed at once if you like. They are all independent of each other, but they try to follow certain standards so that they work in similar ways.

There are also many tools, addons and **plugins** that can installed to make your browser more powerful. For example you can change which **search engine** your browser uses as the default when you use the search bar.

Google Search: Firefox Addons

All of these are freely available for **download**.
Firefox: http://www.mozilla.com/en-US/firefox/personal.html
Google Chrome: http://www.google.com/chrome
Internet Explorer: http://www.microsoft.com/windows/Internet-explorer/default.aspx
Opera: http://www.opera.com/
Safari: http://www.apple.com/safari/

Plugins

Plugins are little pieces of **software** that can be added to your browser to give it more functionality, to make it nice, or generally just to make it better. There are also plugins for looking at certain **files** or website that your browser wouldn't be able to do otherwise. Some of the plugins you may require to view certain files include Adobe Reader for looking at **PDF**s, Adobe Flash Player for websites with flash, Java for websites with small **applications** or applets, and **QuickTime**, **RealPlayer** and Windows Media Player plugins for certain video and audio **online**. They are called plugins because they are "plugged in" to your browser to make it better. They are also generally free to download.

If you come across a site that tells you that you need a plugin to do something, or to continue with what you are doing, they will probably provide you with a way to **install** the plugin. If you don't know if you can trust the website you're on that tells you about this, you can follow the directions below.

Firefox:

Adobe Reader Plugin

> *Google Search*: **Firefox** Adobe Reader Plugin

Mozilla keeps quite an extensive list of **plugins** for Firefox at: https://addons.mozilla.org/en-US/firefox/ -> Categories -> Plugins -> Adobe Reader -> Download Now

Adobe Flash Player Plugin

> *Google Search*: Firefox Adobe Flash Player Plugin

Mozilla keeps quite an extensive list of plugins for Firefox at: https://addons.mozilla.org/en-US/firefox/ -> Categories -> Plugins -> Adobe Flash Player -> Download Now

Java Plugin

> *Google Search*: Firefox Java Plugin

Mozilla keeps quite an extensive list of plugins for Firefox at: https://addons.mozilla.org/en-US/firefox/ -> Categories -> Plugins -> Java -> Download Now

QuickTime Plugin

> *Google Search*: Firefox QuickTime Plugin

Mozilla keeps quite an extensive list of plugins for Firefox at: https://addons.mozilla.org/en-US/firefox/ -> Categories -> Plugins -> QuickTime -> Download Now

Internet Explorer:

Adobe Reader / Adobe Flash Player / Java Plugin

> *Google Search*: Adobe Reader Download
> *Google Search*: Adobe Flash Player
> *Google Search*: Firefox Java Plugin

Having Adobe Reader installed on your system should allow you to open PDFs in Internet Explorer without installing an extra plugin. The same applies to seeing flash with Adobe Flash Player and to applets with Java. If it isn't working, you may have to **install** a newer version of Adobe Reader.

Browser Font Size (Ctrl + '+' or '-')

Font sizes on web pages aren't always optimal. Sometimes it's a single page, and sometimes you just want them all to be larger. You can fix this.

Temporary Size Adjustment

Increase Font Size: Ctrl + '+' (plus sign), repeat until desired size is achieved.

Decrease Font Size: Ctrl + '-' (minus sign), repeat until desired size is achieved.

Go back to the default Font Size: Ctrl + '0' (zero).

Permanent Size Adjustment

Firefox:

"Tools" menu -> "Options..."

Select the  tab.

In the "Fonts & Colors" section, there is an "Advanced" button, which brings up another box. In there is a section labeled "Minimum font size," set that to a larger number then hit "OK" on this box and the other one.

Google Chrome:

No good option for permanent change.

Internet Explorer:

View -> Text Size -> Larger (or Largest)

Opera:

"Tools" -> "Preferences..." -> "Advanced" tab (at the top right) -> "Fonts" section (on the left side)
There is a section labeled "Minimum font size (pixels)," set that to a larger number then hit "OK".

Safari:

"Edit" -> "Preferences…"

Select the  Advanced tab.

Next to "Universal Access:" check the box that says "Never use font sizes smaller than" and set that number larger.

Refresh a Webpage (F5)

If you know a **webpage** is out of date, or you just want to force your **browser** to check for new information, if there is any, you can click the refresh button, or hit F5. The refresh button normally looks like an arrow or two drawn in a circle and is toward the top left of a browser. This can also help if a webpage gets stuck and won't finish loading.

Stop Loading a Webpage (ESC)

Sometimes pages take too long to load, or you click on something you didn't actually want. You can stop the page from loading by hitting ESC (escape key) or the 'Stop Loading' button. This button looks similar to the close button, but it is located right next to the Refresh button, and sometimes it is the refresh button (only while a page is loading).

The 'Stop Loading' button is grayed out when the page has finished loading in **FireFox**, and it is the Refresh button when it has finished loading in **Opera** and **Safari**. There is no button for **Google Chrome**. You can also just hit the **back button** to go back to where you were before you clicked.

Your Homepage (Alt + Home: Most Browsers; Ctrl + Shift + H: Safari)

You can go back to your **homepage** at any point by using these buttons (Firefox, Internet Explorer and Opera only). You can also get to your homepage by opening a new browser window, or using the **shortcut** keys specified above. The 'home' key on your **keyboard** is in the group directly above the arrow keys.

Your **homepage** is the webpage that is loaded automatically when you open your **browser**. You can set your homepage to any webpage or group of web pages you want. Just open the page you want to be your homepage, or open several pages using **tabbed browsing**. Then do the following depending on your browser.

Firefox:

> "Tools" -> "Options..."
> The box that comes up will have a label for "Home Page" next to a box, with a button for "Use Current Pages" directly beneath it. Click that button, then hit OK.

Google Chrome: 🌐

> Sets up a homepage for you using your 9 most visited websites automatically.

Internet Explorer: 🌐

> 🏠 ▾ (downward arrow next to home **icon**) -> "Add or Change Home Page"
>
> or
>
> "Tools" -> "Options..."
> There is a section for Home page with a house icon and a button that says "Use current."
> "Apply" -> "OK"

Opera: 🔴

> "Tools" -> "Preferences..."
> There is a line for Home page, click "Use Current."

Safari:

"Edit" -> "Preferences…"
There is a section for Home page, click "Set to Current Page"

Website Homepage

Homepage can also be used in reference to a particular website. In this case it is the page where you normally begin on a website, or the front door. It's the page that helps you find what you're looking for and shows you what the site is all about. It is different from your **browser** homepage, which is any page you choose to have your browser load automatically for you.

All well-designed sites have an easy way to get back to the **homepage** from anywhere within the site, and it is most often in the top left corner of your browsing window. Sometimes it is just a normal **link** with the name of the site, and sometimes it is the websites logo set up as a link to take you back to the homepage. This makes it less likely that you will get lost on a site, because you always know the way back to the homepage.

Tabbed Browsing

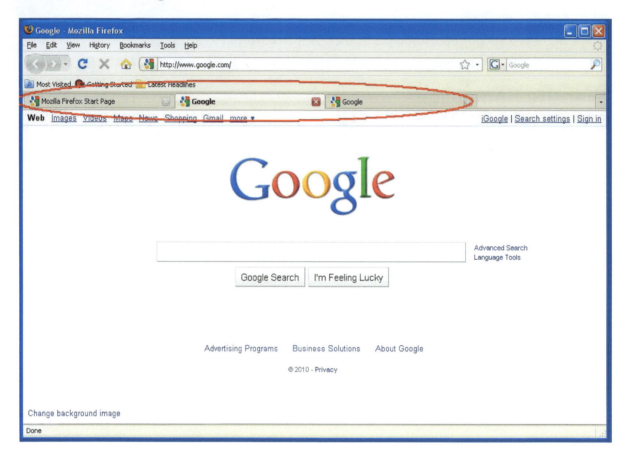

The world of Internet browsers has advanced quite a bit since the beginning of the **Internet**. One of the many ways that life has become easier, is using tabs instead of separate windows for every web page you want to look at. You already have your taskbar full of other things you're doing. No need to fill your taskbar with five copies of **Internet Explorer**, each with a different webpage open. Instead you can have one copy of Internet Explorer open with the five web pages open in five different tabs along the top of the screen under the **address bar**.

Bookmarks/Favorites

Using this function, you can revisit sites you visit frequently without typing the **URL** every time. Some **browsers** call these bookmarks, some call them favorites, so we'll use them interchangeably. Either way they're just **shortcuts** to places on the **Internet**.

Saving a Bookmark

While on a page you would like to save as a bookmark:

Firefox:

Ctrl + D

_or_

"Bookmarks" -> "Bookmark This Page"

Google Chrome:

(The star **icon** to the left of the **address bar**.)

Internet Explorer:

Favorites -> "Add to Favorites…"

_or_

"Favorites" -> "Add to Favorites…"

Opera:

Ctrl + D

_or_

"Bookmarks" -> "Bookmark Page…"

_or_

(Panels button) -> (Bookmark tab) -> Add (Add bookmark button)

Safari:

Ctrl + D

_or_

"Bookmarks" -> "Add Bookmark…"

Organizing Bookmarks

Bookmarks can be sorted into **folders** to make it easier to find them in the future. This is especially helpful if you have a lot of web pages you want to remember.

Firefox:

Ctrl + Shift + B

or

"Bookmarks" -> "Organize Bookmarks…"

Google Chrome:

Ctrl + Shift + B

or

-> "Bookmark manager"

Internet Explorer:

"Favorites" -> "Organize Favorites…"

Opera:

Ctrl + Shift + B

_or_

"Bookmarks" -> "Manage Bookmarks…"

Safari:

Ctrl + Alt + B

_or_

"Bookmarks" -> "Show All Bookmarks"

Exporting Bookmarks

Exporting your bookmarks is a good way to make a backup of them so that you don't lose track of all your favorite websites should something happen to your computer. If this is a concern of yours, you can export a **file** with your bookmarks in it, and **e-mail** it to yourself. It will normally be named something like bookmarks.html or bookmark.html. This '.html' file can be used to import your bookmarks into any **browser**. Also, since it is an .html **document**, you can view it in any browser, which will just show it as a list of **links**.

Firefox:

"Bookmarks" -> "Organize Bookmarks…" or Ctrl + Shift + B

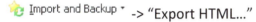 -> "Export HTML…"
Save the .html file to a location of your choice.

Google Chrome:

No option for this.

Internet Explorer:

"File" -> "Import and Export…"
Chose to "Export to a file"
Save the .html file to a location of your choice.

Opera:

"File" -> "Import and Export" -> "Export Bookmarks as HTML…"
Save the .html file to a location of your choice.

Safari:

"File" -> "Export Bookmarks…"
Save the .html file to a location of your choice.

Importing Bookmarks

Firefox:

Import From Another Browser

"File" -> "Import…" -> Select the Browser to import from -> "Next" -> "Next" -> "Finish"

Import From an HTML File

(Ctrl + Shift + B) or "Bookmarks" -> "Organize Bookmarks…"

-> "Import HTML…"
Then choose a browser or file to import from.

Google Chrome:

-> "Import bookmarks & settings…"
This box gives you the option to import bookmarks and other settings from another browser.

Internet Explorer:

"File" -> "Import and Export…"
Choose whether to import from a browser or a file -> "Next"
Choose a browser or file -> "Import" -> "Finish"

Opera:

"File" -> "Import and Export" -> "Import Netscape/Firefox Bookmarks…"
Locate the .html bookmarks file.

Safari:

"File" -> "Import Bookmarks…"
Locate the .html bookmarks file.

Deleting History/Cache/Offline Files/Cookies

The **history** in the browser normally shows itself in a couple of ways. The first is the **address bar**. The down arrow on the right side of the address bar has a list of websites you have visited recently, or you visit often. These are stored in the history. The **forward** and **back buttons** are the second. When you click forward or back, the browser looks in the history to figure out where to go. There is also an arrow to the right of the forward and back button that stores pages you have clicked through recently.

This isn't something that needs to be done often. You should remember that some things that your **browser** normally remembers for you, such as **passwords**, could go away if you do this. This isn't a big deal because it will begin remembering things again immediately afterward. If you have enough space on your **hard drive**, and your browser seems to be running ok, this should probably be left alone.

If your browser seems to be taking longer than it should on a regular basis, or you're having trouble loading certain pages, or images that you know you should be able to, this is something to try. Also, if you're browsing or checking **e-mail** on a computer that isn't your own it is best to clear the **history** when you're done so that your information isn't left there for someone else to find.

Firefox:

(Ctrl + Shift + Delete) or "Tools" -> "Clear Recent History..."
Select "Everything" from the top drop down box, then click "Clear Now."

You can also delete single items in the **Address bar** history by highlighting them with the **mouse** and pressing delete.

Google Chrome:

(Ctrl + Shift + Delete) or [icon] -> "Clear Browsing Data..."
Select "Everything" from the drop down box at the bottom, then click "Clear Browsing Data."

Internet Explorer:

(Ctrl + Shift + Delete) or "Tools" -> "Delete Browsing History..."
click "Delete."

You can also delete single items in the Address bar history by highlighting them with the mouse and pressing the small "X" that appears.

Opera:

"Tools" -> "Delete Private Data..."
click "Delete"

Safari:

"History" -> "Clear History"
"Edit" -> "Empty Cache..." -> "Empty"

Understanding Website Addresses

We will use
http://www.google.com/
http://maps.google.com/

http://www.msn.com/
http://www.aol.com/
http://www.eddiemc.com/about.html

as examples. These show how the addresses would appear in the **address bar** if you were on the website.

http://

The "**http**" stands for **HyperText Transfer Protocol**, which basically just tells the **browser** and the **server** how to talk to each other. These days the **Internet** and browsers are smarter, so it isn't necessary to type in the "http://" part of the address anymore for most websites. This is the default if you don't specify anything. There are other values that could go in this spot like "https://" which is http secure, and "ftp://" which is for transferring **files**.

www

The "www" says that the website is on the World Wide Web. This can normally be omitted when typing an address in the address bar. For example, an alias for "www.eddiemc.com" is "eddiemc.com" so that is all you have to type to get to my webpage.

Domain Extension

The "com" says that the website is on the commercial domain. This is referred to as a "Domain Extension." The Domain Extension is always after the last dot. There are a lot of extensions on the World Wide Web. Some of the most common are:

.com - Commercial, used by businesses and individuals
.net - Network, used by some **Internet** related companies, and as an alternative to .com
.edu - Educational, only educational institutions use this domain
.org - Organizational, typically used by non-profit groups, or as an alternative to .com or .net
.gov - Government, only used for US government related websites

All of these are U.S. only domains. This just means that they must exist inside of the U.S., but they can normally be accessed from anywhere. There are also two letter extensions for Countries like:

.fr - France
.ie - Ireland
.jp - Japan
.us - United States

Website Name

The part directly before the domain extension is the website. The websites listed above are "Google," "MSN," "AOL," and "eddiemc". Anything located before these names, and after the "www" or "http://" are parts of a larger website. Above "maps.google.com" is just a piece of the larger site known as "google.com." An important note to make here is that www.google.false.com (not a real website) is not the same as www.false.google.com (also not a real webpage). The first one is actually under the false.com domain and has nothing to do with Google. I mention this because some scammers have been known to use this method to trick users into logging into their website and giving away **usernames** and **passwords**. Just imagine if that was your bank's website instead of Google.

Web Page

Web sites are contained in **folders** on a computer somewhere just like **files** on your own computer. These just happen to be a **server** that allows you to see the files.

Everything after the domain extension of a **URL** leads to the actual webpage. If you're on the default **homepage** for a website, the webpage name sometimes is just left off because it is assumed to be index.html, welcome.html, or home.html. This means that "www.eddiemc.com/" is the same as "www.eddiemc.com/index.html".

For "www.eddiemc.com/about.html" you're on the "about.html" page, which can also just be called the "about" page. There could have been other folders between the domain extension and the webpage. For example we could have "www.eddiemc.com/eddie/recent/about.html" which is still the "about" page, but it is contained within the "recent" folder which is contained within the "eddie" folder.

Downloading

There are lots of sites that allow you to **download** content from **programs** and music to files and pictures. When you download these files, they are stored onto your own computer.

Chapter 7 – E-mail

E-mail Providers

The major reason that people use different **e-mail** services is just based on preferences and what they like better. E-mail can be used on a website as mentioned below or on your computer if you use a **program** like **Outlook Express**, or Thunder Bird. These programs connect to the **Internet** so you can retrieve your e-mails and store them directly on your computer.

The most popular e-mail websites as of this writing are:

- Gmail
- Yahoo Mail
- Hotmail
- AIM/AOL Mail

Sending Web Pages

It's nice to be able to share web pages with other people. Most of the time, you can just copy the text in the **address bar** in your **browser** while it is on the web page and paste it in the e-mail you want to send.

As an example we will send an AOL news article. The AOL News page contains quite a few introductions for news articles with a small blurb about the article and sometimes a picture. Typically these have a **link** for the "Full Story" at the bottom left of the article description.

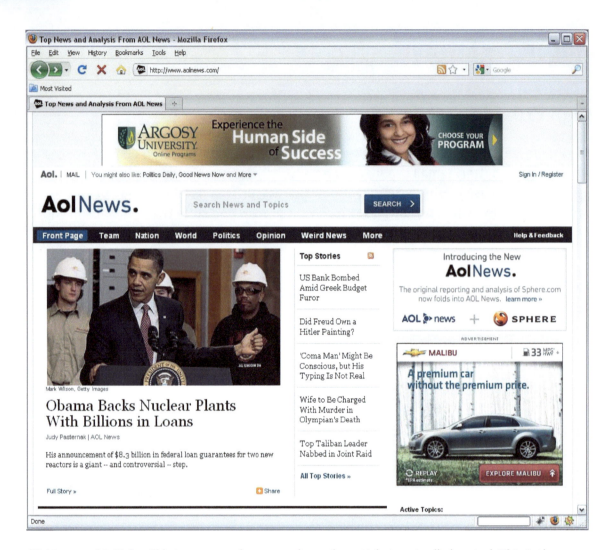

Clicking on this **link** will bring you to the page where the article is actually located. This is the page that can be sent to someone else so that they can read the article. Sending the outer www.aolnews.com page doesn't always work because this is one of the many pages on the **Internet** that is constantly updated. This means that it won't look the same tomorrow as it does today.

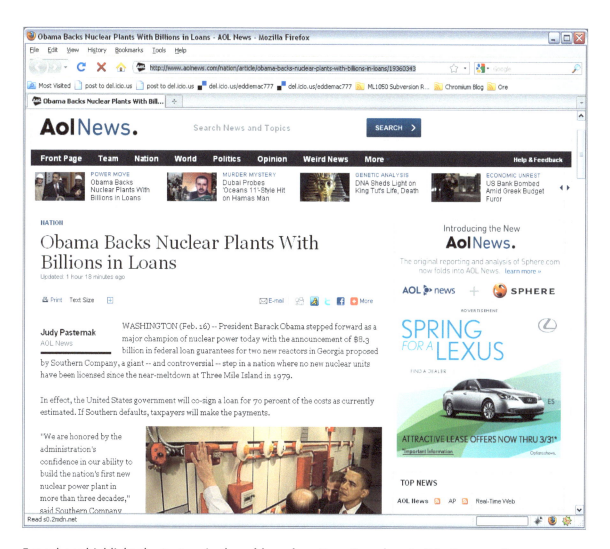

From here highlight the text up in the **address bar**. Copy it, and paste it in the **e-mail** you want to send.

Webpage Links

Some websites have e-mail addresses on their site that you can click on to send them an e-mail, but this click brings up a **program** on your computer for sending the e-mail. This will normally be something like **Outlook Express** or **Thunderbird**. If you don't use these programs, this isn't helpful for you. If one of these programs does open up, there will be an e-mail address listed in the "To" field. Just select that address with your **mouse** and copy it. You can then open up your own e-mail and paste it in the "To" field. Refer to **Chapter 4** if you need more details about this.

Be careful about **links** to websites inside of e-mails. It is safer to copy and paste the link into your address bar, or type it yourself. This is a good way to thwart **phishers** who try to trick you to go their website, which looks exactly like the site you want, so that they can get information from you.

Blocked Pictures

These will show up as small squares or rectangles in **e-mail**s you receive. Sometimes they won't show up at all, but there will be a warning message. They're blocked for security reasons, but if you know and trust the sender you can unblock these pictures so that you can see the full e-mail.

You can tell that pictures in an e-mail have been blocked by something like this toward the top of the e-mail in question:

AIM Mail -

> Enable links: for this message | always for this sender

Click "for this message" to see **links** and images for this e-mail only.
Click "always for this sender" to never block links and images from a particular sender again.

Gmail -

> **Images are not displayed.**
> Display images below - Always display images from

Click "Display images below" to see them for this e-mail only.
Click "Always display images from ..." to never block images from a particular sender again.

Hotmail -

> Attachments, pictures, and links in this message have been blocked for your safety.   Show content

Click "Show content" to see the images.

Yahoo Mail -

Go to Options -> Mail Options

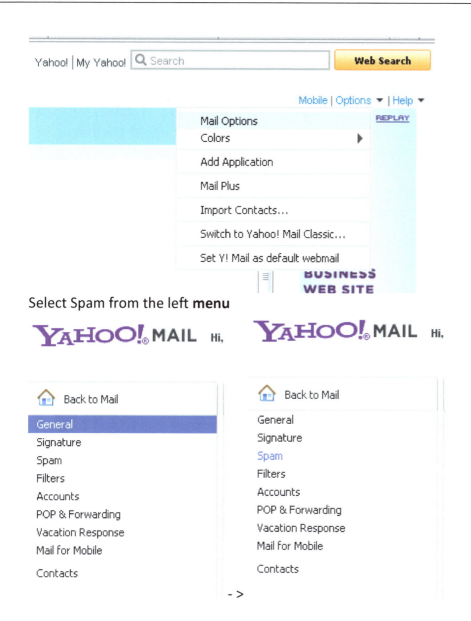

Select Spam from the left **menu**

-->

In the SpamGuard section, you can either choose to "Always show images, except in Spam folder", or "Show images only from my contacts."

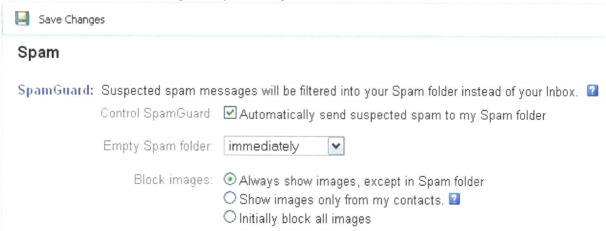

MAILER-DAEMON

Whenever you send an **e-mail** that doesn't go through properly, you get back a message from the Mail Delivery Subsystem that has a lot of information in it. Normally this is because the recipient's name was typed in wrong or they don't exist. If you re-check that information, you can normally fix the problem yourself.

You don't have to read these messages except the part that tells you which address you couldn't send to (or contact), which is normally toward the top and on its own line.

Carbon Copy (CC)

This field is used to tell people that they aren't the main or only recipient of an e-mail. It could be that you were sending an e-mail to a co-worker, and you wanted your boss to see it, but not feel the need to respond to it. In this case you could put your co-worker's e-mail address in the 'To' field, and your bosses e-mail address in the 'CC' field.

Blind Carbon Copy (BCC)

If you want to send an e-mail to several people, but don't want them to see each other's e-mail addresses, you should use BCC. For instance sending the same e-mail to several people who don't know each other, or sending to a large number of recipients who should only reply to you and not each other. Maybe you just want someone to see the e-mail that you're sending to someone else. In these cases, you should put e-mail addresses in the BCC section of the e-mail. No one on the receiving side will see any of the addresses that were in the BCC field.

Attachments

Attachments can be very useful for e-mailing **documents** to people, but typically **programs** and **executables** are not allowed as attachments because of security issues. In general things like pictures, documents, **spreadsheets** and **pdf files** are acceptable for attaching to an e-mail. E-mail providers have different limits to how large a file can be; it is 25MB for gmail right now. If it is too large, they won't allow you to attach it, or they will warn you that it is too large and won't send it.

You should also keep in mind that the larger the file, the longer it will take the intended recipient to **download** and open it. As a general rule I like to make sure that attachments will be smaller than 10 **MB**. If you really need to send something larger than this, you can compress it, or break it up into pieces. There are also websites that will allow you to upload **files** so that you can just **e-mail** the **link** to others.

Attaching a File

In order to send a file to someone else, you must attach it in the e-mail you're sending to them.

AIM Mail -

Click the "Attach" button. Then locate the file you want to attach and click "Open."

Gmail -

Subject:

 Attach a file

Click "Attach a file" with the paperclip next to it. Then locate the file you want to attach and click "Open."

Hotmail -

Send   Save draft   Attach   Spell check

Click the "Attach" portion of the menu bar that is located toward the top of your e-mail, just above your **username**. This will add a box labeled "Browse" just below the Subject line.

Subject:

Browse…

Click on "Browse" and locate the file you want to attach then click "Open."

Yahoo Mail -

Subject:

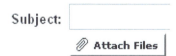 Attach Files

Click on the "Attach Files" button below the subject line, which will bring up a new window for selecting your files.

Click on the "Browse" button next to "File 1" and locate the **file** you wish to attach, then press "Open." Do this for all files you wish to attach.

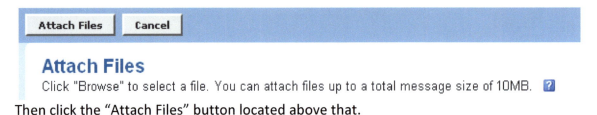

Then click the "Attach Files" button located above that.

Saving a File from Attachment

If you want to keep a received attached file, you must save it to your computer. In most cases the filenames are colored blue to indicate that you may click on them to perform some action.

AIM Mail -

Click on the **link** with the file name next to the paperclip. Then make sure that the "Save File" option is selected if there is one and press "OK" or "Save."

Gmail -

Click on the word "Download" to the right of the file you want to save. Then make sure the "Save File" option is selected if there is one and press "OK" or "Save."

Hotmail -

📎 1 attachment
   TextFile1...txt (0.1 KB)

Click on the filename you wish to save from the **attachment**. Then make sure that the "Save File" option is selected if there is one and press "OK" or "Save."

Yahoo Mail - 🅨!

📎   TextFile1.txt (73b)

Click on the text of the filename you wish to save from the attachment.

📎   TextFile1.txt (73b)

No virus threat detected File: TextFile1.txt   Download File

Then click on the "Download File" text that appears if a box hasn't already popped up for saving. Then make sure that the "Save File" option is selected if there is one and press "OK" or "Save."

E-mail Etiquette

It is common courtesy not to **e-mail** or post anything on the **Internet** in all capital letters. This is viewed as yelling, and it is more difficult to read. If you want to get your point across, you should try another method, like possibly well written sentences with explicit statements about your thoughts on the matter. Also, sarcasm doesn't really work in writing. On the Internet people can't see your facial expressions or hear the tone of your voice, so they are less likely to perceive your disdain for something if it is sarcastic.

Chapter 8 – Simple Troubleshooting

These are some easy things you can try before calling someone when things aren't working like they're supposed to.

Network

There are a lot of reasons that your **Internet** could not be working, these are just a few of the ways you may be able to get it running again. **Dial-up** is fading fast because of new technology, and it really isn't very efficient, so I'm not even going to mention it here.

Hardware

First and most important, make sure all of your wires are connected and everything is on. Network setups will be different in most situations, but in general you will have a **modem** connected to the "Internet" and the **router** connected to your computer(s).

Modem

If you don't seem to be getting Internet anywhere in your house; no other computers can access the Internet either, then you can try rebooting your modem.

Just unplug the power to the modem for a minute or so, then plug it back in and wait. Let it sit for a minute or so. If your Internet still doesn't seem to be working check the router next.

Router

If rebooting your modem doesn't help, you can try the same thing with your router (if you have one). If you only have one computer in your house, you may not have a router.

Just unplug the power to the router for about a minute, then plug it back in and wait a minute. If your Internet still doesn't seem to be working, you can go up to the **software** section and try some of those steps.

Software

One thing worth trying if nothing else seems to work is to **reboot** your computer. Sometime it will know how to fix itself as long as everything else is working properly.

Windows XP

Wired connection:

Down in the taskbar there is an **icon** with a picture of two computers that will cycle as lit and unlit when the **network** is working properly. Something like this:

▉->▉->▉->▉->▉->▉->▉->▉->▉

If it is not working, or you have no **Internet**, it will probably show up with and "X" through it. Right-click on that icon and select "Repair."

If that doesn't work, you can also **reboot** your computer to let it try to establish network connections again on its own.

Monitor

Hardware

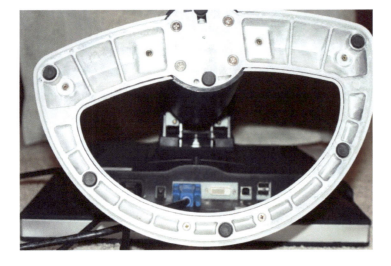 

The first and most important thing to check is that your cords are plugged into the monitor correctly. There should be a power cord that runs from the back of the monitor to a socket. Make sure both ends are properly connected, if you can't tell just unplug both ends and plug them back in.

The other cord in the back of the monitor is the one that gets the signal from your computer. Some monitors have this cable permanently attached. If the end attached to the monitor isn't permanent, make sure it isn't loose. If it is, there are two finger screws on it that you can tighten. The end that attaches to the computer also has finger screws that can be tightened if it is loose.

Make sure the monitor power is on using the power button on the monitor. Most power buttons light up when they are on.

CD/DVD Drive

If your CD or **DVD drive** is stuck and won't open, or if your computer is off, but you need to get a disk out, this method can help you out. There is a small, almost unnoticeable hole on the front face of almost all CD and DVD drives. Just straighten out the end of a paperclip and press gently straight into the hole. When you do this the drive should release its lock and open just slightly. From there you can use your fingers to open it the rest of the way.

[The Manual That Didn't Come With Your Computer (but should have)]   McWhirter

Chapter 9 – Security

Security is important for your computer because not everyone on the **Internet** is trustworthy. There will be people who try to **crash** your computer or steal your information, so it is important to keep things up to date.

Operating System

Windows XP

There is an option to have automatic updates put on your computer. Go to Start -> Control Panel -> Security Center -> Automatic Updates

If you don't know anything about any of this and don't want to mess with it, just choose the first option: Automatic (recommended)

If you want to make sure you know about updates, and you're **always connected** to the Internet, but don't want Windows telling you to restart your computer all the time when you're not ready to do so, choose the second option: Download updates for me, but let me choose when to **install** them.
With this option, the little yellow shield **icon** will appear in the taskbar whenever there are new updates to install. Just click on it when you're ready to **download** and install them.

If you don't want be notified, but want to do all the work yourself, choose: Notify me but don't automatically download or install them.

If you want to do it all yourself, just choose: Turn off Automatic Updates. This is the least secure option by far.

I like to use the second setting myself ("Download updates for me, but let me choose when to install them").

Firewall

Firewalls help to keep out some of the bad **programs** that are always trying to break you're your machine on the Internet. Windows XP comes with a firewall. One option is to turn that one on.
Go to Start -> Control Panel -> Security Center -> Windows Firewall
or
Go to Start -> Control Panel -> Windows Firewall

| 9BChapter 9 – Security   95

Then click 'On (recommended)' and click 'OK'.

Anti-Virus

All computers should have some sort of **Anti-Virus** installed and up to date, especially if you're using Windows. There are quite a few viable options for this. Some of them are free, some of them have a subscription for updates, and some of them even have an initial cost. You should definitely have Anti-Virus **software** on your computer and up to date if you ever connect to the **Internet**. You only need one Anti-Virus **program** on your computer. Having more than one can sometimes cause problems with the two conflicting with each other.

Be sure to check the websites for specific software for more details.

AVG

> **Download** it on their website: http://free.avg.com/us-en/homepage

> Compatible with: Windows XP, Windows Vista, and Windows 7

> The free version of this contains just the anti-virus and **anti-spyware** parts of the program. You can pay to get more tools that help with other security issues if you think you need them. You can buy these on their website. I use the free version on my personal computer downloaded from their website.

Norton

> Buy it on their website: http://www.symantec.com/norton/antivirus
> The software can be downloaded here as well if you purchase **online**.

> Compatible with: Windows XP, Windows Vista, and Windows 7

> Written by **Symantec**, this is a subscription based anti-virus and anti-spyware package. You can pay more to get the more extensive Internet security packages here as well, if you feel you need the extra security. Subscriptions are typically yearly.

McAfee

> Buy it on their website: http://home.mcafee.com/Store/Downloads.aspx

> Compatible with: Windows XP, Windows Vista, Windows 7

> A subscription based anti-virus and anti-spyware package. They have several different options if you're looking for more security. Subscriptions are typically yearly.

Anti-Spyware

The **anti-virus** programs mentioned above include **anti-spyware** capabilities. The **programs** below are specifically for anti-spyware purposes. Be sure to check their websites for more details.

Ad-aware

Download it on their website: http://www.lavasoft.com/

Compatible with: Windows XP, Windows Vista, Windows 7

Written by Lavasoft, this is an anti-spyware package that includes **malware (anti-malware)** protection. You can buy versions that come with anti-virus protection and support. I use the free version on my personal computer downloaded from their website.

Spybot Search & Destroy

Download on their website: http://www.safer-networking.org/en/spybotsd/

Compatible with: Windows XP, Windows Vista, Windows 7, **Linux** (with Wine)

This is an anti-spyware package. I use this on my personal computer.

E-mail

Don't trust **e-mails** from people you don't know. If you don't know them, definitely don't open anything attached to an e-mail they sent you. There are hoaxes and **phishing** scams everywhere, don't trust everyone or everything you see out there.

Links in E-mails

If you click on a **link** in an e-mail, make sure that it takes you where you think it is taking you. Look in the **address bar**, and refer to Chapter 5 for more details. As a safer option, you can copy and paste the link into the address bar, or just type it yourself.

E-mail Address Specifics

When you get an e-mail there is an e-mail address in the "From:" field that signifies who sent the message to you.

They generally come in the form:
  Computer Helper <computer.help.book@gmail.com>

The part between the brackets (<>) is the actual **e-mail** address:
  computer.help.book@gmail.com

The part before the '@' is the **username** chosen by the user: computer.help.book

This username can be any combination of letters, numbers, underscores (_), and periods(.). It must begin with a letter.

The part after the '@' states who is providing the e-mail service: gmail.com

Other common possibilities for this are: hotmail.com, yahoo.com, aol.com, and comcast.com

The section before the brackets can be anything the user specifies: Computer Helper

This is important to note, and this is how some spammers trick users into following their e-mails. Since this can be anything, they can make it say "support@amazon.net" even though their actual e-mail address is <dirtyliar@nothonest.com>. Make sure you always look at the e-mail address listed between the brackets if you're not sure who sent you the e-mail.

Another way to pick out **spam** from real e-mails is to look at the "To:" field. If it shows something similar to your e-mail address, but not exactly the same, it is probably spam. Most e-mail providers have spam blockers, but check the "spam" **folder** if you're waiting for an e-mail. Sometimes real e-mails can be marked as spam.

Shopping Online

If you're going to place orders **online**, make sure that you do it through a website you know and trust. This just makes sense.

Don't give out your information in e-mails or chats. Only submit your credit card information on secure websites (they usually have a little lock showing at the bottom of the screen).

Chapter 10 – Computer Maintenance

There several different things you can do to make sure your computer is in peak condition. Some of them are **software** related and will be done while your computer is on. Some are **hardware** related and will be done while your computer is off.

Cleaning Up Your Hard Drive

Just using your computer will cause your **hard drive** to get cluttered and possibly begin to slow down or even fill up. This is partly due to **files** that are **downloaded** or saved in random location that you don't use anymore. It is also partially due to how your computer saves files in random locations on your hard drive.

Windows XP

Startup Folder

If your computer seems to be taking longer than it used to while starting up it may be because a lot of **programs** are loading when you load Windows. These normally aren't necessary, and just slow things down. Removing things from the startup **folder** doesn't mean you can't use them anymore. You will just have to load them yourself by double-clicking on them. In my opinion there shouldn't be more than one or two items in this folder that you just use all the time.

Go to Start -> All Programs -> Startup
Right-click on any items you want to remove and select 'Delete.'

While you're in here you can also sort the **Start Menu** alphabetically by right-clicking anywhere inside of the 'All Programs' area and selecting 'Sort by Name.' If you want to organize further, you'll notice that you can drag items around and put them in different places within the Start Menu.

Disk Error-Checking

I don't do this more than once or twice a year, but if your computer is acting funny and you don't know what else to do, it doesn't hurt to try.

Go to "My Computer" right-click on "Local Disk (C:)" -> Properties. Go to the "Tools" tab.

Click "Check Now..." in the section for "Error-checking."

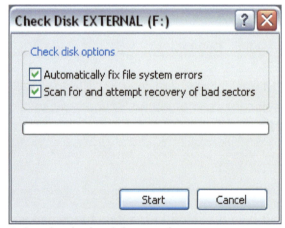

Select both check boxes shown:

"Automatically fix file system errors" and

"Scan for and attempt recovery of bad sectors"

Then click "Start." Windows will ask if you want to schedule the scan for the next time you restart your machine (If you selected the C: drive; I'm using another drive in my example). You should click 'yes' here, but be warned that this can take quite a while once your computer is rebooted. It won't however **reboot** automatically; it will wait until the next time the computer starts up. I would recommend doing it at night before you go to bed and just letting it run overnight.

This same tool can be used on other **hard drives** as well if you have them.

Disk Defragmenter

The way that Windows creates and deletes **files** causes files to be stored randomly all over your hard drive. If your computer starts to feel sluggish when you're trying to access files, this is something to try. I normally run the **defragmenter** about once a month just to keep things in order and running smoothly.

Go to "My Computer" right-click on "Local Disk (C:)" -> Properties. Go to the "Tools" tab.

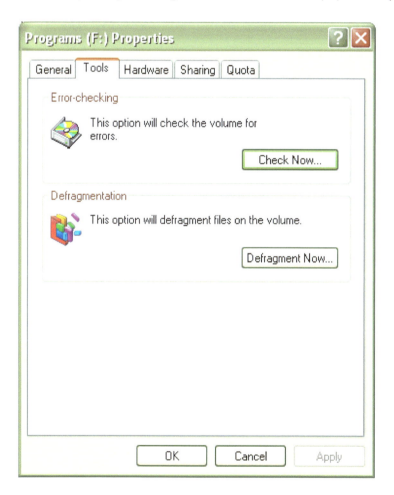

Click "Defragment Now..." in the "Defragmentation" section. Select your "(C:)" drive at the top, then press the "Defragment" button. This can take anywhere from a couple of minutes to a couple of hours, but Windows will keep you updated with how far along it is.

This same tool can be used on other **hard drives** as well if you have them. Just select them instead of the C drive in the **Defragmenter** list.

Remove Unused Programs

Be careful to only remove things that you have installed, and that you don't want or use anymore.

To remove a **program** you don't want any more go to the Control Panel and select "Add or Remove Programs." Search through the list to find the program and highlight it with the **mouse**. A "Remove" button will show up on the right side. Just click that and follow the instructions.

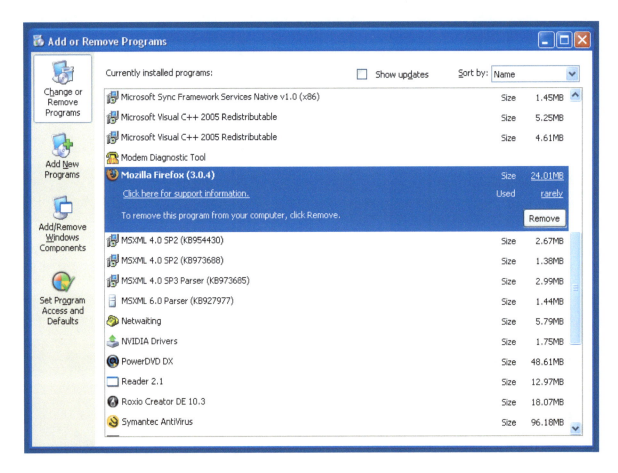

Windows Vista

Disk Error-Checking

Go to Start -> Computer, then right-click on "Local Disk (C:)" -> Properties. Go to the "Tools" tab. Click "Check Now..." in the section for "Error-checking." Select both check boxes shown:
   "Automatically fix file system errors" and
   "Scan for and attempt recovery of bad sectors"

Then click "Start." Windows will almost always ask if you want to schedule the scan for the next time you restart your machine. You should click 'yes' here, but be warned that this can take quite a while. I would recommend doing it at night before you go to bed and just letting it run overnight.

Cleaning Your Mouse

This is only really necessary if your mouse doesn't seem to be moving properly, or if it just looks really dirty.

Quick and Dirty

Just flip your mouse over and look at the pads. If there is a buildup of gunk just scrape if off with the top of your fingernail, or a mechanical pencil without lead. As long as there isn't anything sticky on your desk or mouse, it should come off fairly easily.

Thorough

1. Unplug the mouse from your computer. It is probably best to do this while the computer is off.
2. Follow the directions for the *Quick and Dirty* section.
3. Get a wash cloth and some rubbing alcohol (Isopropyl 70% is what I use).
4. Hold the wash cloth over the opened top of the bottle of Isopropyl Alcohol and tip it sideways to dampen a small spot on the wash cloth.

5. Use the damp portion of the wash cloth to rub the dirt and gunk off of the buttons and pads on the bottom.

6. If the cloth gets too dirty, just dampen another spot on the cloth and repeat as necessary until clean.
7. It should dry very quickly, but make sure it is completely dry before plugging it back into the computer.

Cleaning Your Keyboard

This is only necessary if keys on your **keyboard** are sticking or sticky. You can also do this if it just looks really dirty.

Quick and Dirty

Just flip the keyboard upside-down while it is over a trash can or outside and shake it. You may need to unplug it from the computer to do this. Most of the loose debris between the keys should fall out.

Thorough

1. Unplug the keyboard from your computer. It is probably best to do this while the computer is off.
2. Follow the directions for the *Quick and Dirty* section.
3. Optional: Use a can of compressed air to blow out any other debris from between the keys. Make sure the can of air is always right side up. It is probably best to do this outside, or away from other things you don't want to get dirty. If you don't have compressed air, use a vacuum, but make sure to use an attachment small enough that if any keys fall off, they don't get sucked up.
4. Get a wash cloth and some rubbing alcohol (Isopropyl 70% is what I use).
5. Hold the wash cloth over the opened top of the bottle of Isopropyl Alcohol and tip it sideways to dampen a small spot on the wash cloth.

6. Use the damp portion of the wash cloth to rub the dirt and gunk off of the keys and the edges of the keyboard.

7. If the cloth gets too dirty, just dampen another spot on the cloth and repeat as necessary until clean.

8. Once the tops of the keys are clean you can use a q-tip dipped in the Isopropyl Alcohol to clean between the keys. Only dip one side of the q-tip in the Alcohol then press it against the side of the bottle to let the excess drip off, it only needs to be damp. Use the damp side of the q-tip to clean between keys and the dry side to dry between each key.

9. It should dry very quickly, but make sure it is completely dry before plugging it back into the computer.

You can follow the same general procedure for laptops, but make sure to unplug it, turn it off and take out the battery first. Then make sure it is completely dry before you put the battery back in and plug it in.

Chapter 11 - Extension Help

If everything is working properly, you won't ever have to think about this, but sometimes it's just not that easy. When you open a **file** it should open automatically in the default **program**. If it doesn't this list will help you find the proper program. They are alphabetical by **extension**. Remember that the extension is the last 3 or 4 letters of the filename, and it will always be after a period. The extension tells your computer what program to use for a file and what format the file is saved in.

Show File Extensions

Windows XP

Inside of any **folder** or My Computer go to Tools -> Folder Options... then go to the "View" tab. Uncheck the box that says "Hide extensions for known file types" then click the "Apply to All Folders" button.

Extension List

This is not a complete list, just some of the more common file types. If a file doesn't open automatically, you can right click, go to '*open with*' and see if any of these programs are in the list. If not, you may need to find and **install** one. Extensions are not case sensitive in Windows, so .txt is the same as .TXT.

Also note that Windows Picture and Fax Viewer () is just a default viewer in Windows that opens pictures when you double-click on them.

.bmp - Any Picture view or editor (**Paint**, Picasa Photo Viewer, Microsoft Office **Picture Manager**, Windows Picture and Fax Viewer, **QuickTime PictureViewer**)

.css – Any **Browser** (**FireFox**, **Internet Explorer**, Netscape, **Opera**, **Safari**) or Text Editor (**Notepad**, WordPad, Microsoft Word, **OpenOffice Writer**). **CSS** files are normally associated with an **HTML** file, so you should not have to open them directly unless you want to change them.

.doc (Microsoft Word **Document**) – Microsoft Word, OpenOffice Writer, Microsoft Word Viewer (Chapter 5)

.docx – Microsoft Word 2007 or higher, Microsoft Word with downloadable extension, Microsoft Word Viewer (Chapter 5)

.exe – This is an **executable**, and should require another **program** to run it. Launching it will either **launch** the program, or **install** if it is an installer.

.gif - Any Picture view or editor (**Paint**, Picasa Photo Viewer, Microsoft Office **Picture Manager**, Windows Picture and Fax Viewer, **QuickTime PictureViewer**)

.htm - Any **Browser** (**FireFox**, **Google Chrome**, **Internet Explorer**, **Opera**, **Safari**)

.html – Any Browser (FireFox, Google Chrome, Internet Explorer, Opera, Safari)

.jpg (JPEG Picture **File**) – Any Picture view or editor (Paint, Picasa Photo Viewer, Microsoft Office Picture Manager, Windows Picture and Fax Viewer, QuickTime PictureViewer)

.mp3 – Any Music Player (**iTunes**, Windows Media Player, **QuickTime**, **RealPlayer**)

.m4a – iTunes, RealPlayer

.mov - QuickTime

.msi – Installer package, launching this will install the program.

.pdf – Adobe Reader, Adobe Acrobat, Firefox

.png - Any Picture view or editor (**Paint**, Picasa Photo Viewer, Microsoft Office Picture Manager, Windows Picture and Fax Viewer, QuickTime PictureViewer)

.pps (Microsoft PowerPoint Presentation) – Microsoft PowerPoint, PowerPoint Viewer (Chapter 5), OpenOffice Impress

.ppt (Microsoft PowerPoint Presentation) – Microsoft PowerPoint, PowerPoint Viewer (Chapter 5), OpenOffice Impress

.pptx (Microsoft PowerPoint Presentations) – Microsoft PowerPoint 2007 or higher, Microsoft PowerPoint with **downloadable** extension, Microsoft PowerPoint Viewer (Chapter 5)

.pub – Microsoft Publisher

.rtf – Microsoft Word, **OpenOffice Writer**

.tif - Paint, Microsoft Office **Picture Manager**

.txt – Any Text Editor (**Notepad**, WordPad, Microsoft Word, **OpenOffice Writer**)

.wav – Any Music Player (**iTunes**, Windows Media Player, **QuickTime**, **RealPlayer**)

.wma – Windows Media Player

.xls (Microsoft **Excel** Spreadsheet) – Microsoft Excel, **OpenOffice Calc**, Microsoft Excel Viewer (Chapter 5)

.xlsx (Microsoft Excel Spreadsheet) – Microsoft Excel 2007 or higher, Microsoft Excel with **downloadable** extension, Microsoft Excel Viewer (Chapter 5)

.xml – Any **Browser** (**FireFox**, **Google Chrome**, **Internet Explorer**, **Opera**, **Safari**)

.zip (Compressed **File**) – WinZip, WinRAR

Chapter 12 – Converting Files

Changing the **extension** on a **file** isn't as easy as renaming it with the last three letters different. The extension represents the kind of **program** that can open a file. If you need to change a file extension, it is necessary to open it with the proper program first.

If you just want to know what program to use to open a file with a particular extension, there is a quick reference for extensions in Chapter 11.

Picture Files

bmp, gif, jpg/jpeg, png, tif/tiff

Method 1 (Windows XP)
Open in Paint, choose File -> Save As
In the "Save as type:" dropdown choose between
- "24-bit Bitmap (*.bmp,*.dib)"
- "GIF (*.GIF)"
- "JPEG (*.JPG,*.JPEG,*JPE,*JFIF)"
- "PNG (*.PNG)"
- "TIFF (*.TIF,*.TIFF)" then click Save.

Method 2 (Windows XP with Microsoft Office)
Open in Microsoft Office Picture Manager, choose File -> Export…
In the "Export with this file format" section to the right choose between
- "Windows Bitmap (*.bmp)"
- "GIF Graphics Interchange Format (*.gif)"
- "JPEG File Interchange Format (*.jpg)"
- "PNG Portable Network Graphics Format (*.png)"
- "TIFF Tag Image File Format (*.tif)"

Chapter 13 – Other Useful Tips

Windows XP

Turn off "Desktop Cleanup Wizard"

Right-click on the **desktop** -> Properties.

Go to the Desktop tab -> "Customize Desktop…"

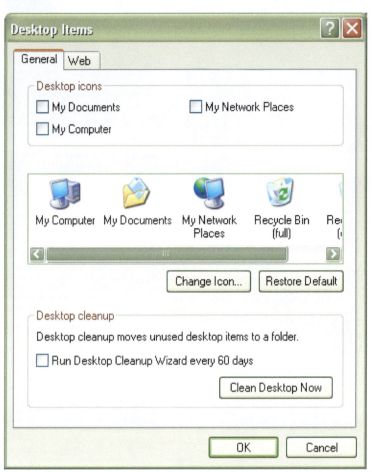

In the "Desktop cleanup" section make sure the box is unchecked for "Run Desktop Cleanup Wizard every 60 days."

To turn on the wizard, just follow the same steps and make sure the box is checked.

Add Account

Start -> Control Panel -> User Accounts -> Create a new Account
Type a name for the new account and click "Next." Select either administrator or limited -> "Create Account"

Delete Account

Start -> Control Panel -> User Accounts
Then select the account to delete -> "Delete the account." Decide whether you want to keep or delete the **files** from the account then click "Delete Account." Keeping files mostly refers to the ones in the "My Documents" **folder** of the selected user.

Change Picture (Avatar)

This is the picture that shows next to your **username** if you use a **login** for your computer on Windows XP home, and it shows up in the **Start Menu**.

Start -> Control Panel -> User Accounts
Then select the account -> "Change my Picture"
Find the picture you want to use, then press "Change Picture"

Change Desktop Image

Right-Click on **Desktop** -> Properties -> Desktop tab

Select an image from the list, or Browse for another one, then press "OK."

Hide/Unhide Taskbar

Right-click on the Taskbar -> check/uncheck "Auto-hide the taskbar" -> "OK"

Screen Saver Settings

Right-Click on **Desktop** -> Properties -> Screen Saver tab

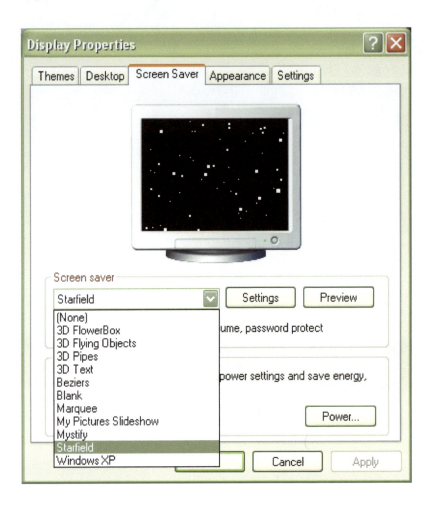

From here you can choose the type of screen saver you want to use, how long your computer will wait with no activity before the brings up the screen saver, and some other settings.

If you'd like to turn the screen saver off select '(None)' from the drop down box.

Conclusion

After I had written over 125 pages of this book, I discovered this series of books with "The Missing Manual" in the title. From what I've seen they are very helpful for the subjects they cover. I've read a few of them now and found them useful. So if you're looking for more information, I would go there next.

Common Keyboard Shortcuts

Keyboard Only

General:
Copy: Ctrl + C (with text or **files** selected)
Cut: Ctrl + X (with text or files selected)
Paste: Ctrl + V (pastes at position of cursor)
Find a word: Ctrl + F
Print: Ctrl + P
Save: Ctrl + S
Select All: Ctrl + A
Undo: Ctrl + Z (if undo is possible)
Redo: Ctrl + Y (undo an undo)
Show **Desktop**: Win Key + D (Windows only)
Minimize All Windows: Windows Key + M
Restore All Minimized Windows: Windows Key + Shift + M
F1: Help file of current selected program
F10: Highlights the menu bar so that you can use the arrow keys instead of the mouse.
Cycle through open programs forward: Alt + Tab
Cycle through open programs backwards: Alt + Shift + Tab
Move to the next field in a form: Tab
Move backwards in a form: Shift + Tab
Shift + Delete: Delete a file without sending it to recycle bin
Ctrl + End: Jump to the last file in a **folder**
Lock Computer: Windows Key + L

General (Windows 7):
Maximize: Windows Key + Up Arrow
Minimize: Windows Key + Down Arrow
Look at Desktop: Windows Key + Hold Space Bar
Zoom In: Windows Key + '+'
Zoom Out: Windows Key + '-'
Minimize all Windows: Windows Key + M
Restore all Windows: Windows Key + Shift + M

Browsers Only:
Ctrl + L: moves cursor up to the **Address Bar** so you can type a **URL**
        (In older versions of **Internet Explorer** this brings up a box with the same purpose.)
F6: moves cursor up to the Address Bar
Ctrl + T: open a new tab

Ctrl + Click: opens **link** in a new tab (if you have a middle button on your mouse, this is the same thing)

Ctrl + W: close the current tab

Ctrl + Shift + T: reopen the last tab that was closed (not Safari)

Ctrl + N: open a new **browser** window

Zoom in: Ctrl + "+"

Zoom out: Ctrl + "-"

Default font size: Ctrl + 0

Back (previous page): Alt + left arrow *or* Backspace *or* Shift + mouse wheel down

Forward (undo back): Alt + right arrow *or* Shift + mouse wheel up

Alt + Home: Go to your **homepage** (not Safari)

Ctrl + Shift + H: Go to your homepage (Safari only)

Ctrl + Shift + Del: Clear Browsing History (not Opera, not Safari)

Ctrl + F: Open the 'Find' tool for searching text.

Ctrl + Tab: Cycle through tabs, forward.

Ctrl + Shift + Tab: Cycle through tabs, backward.

Ctrl + H: Open browsing **history**.

Ctrl + D: Add current page to bookmarks/favorites

Microsoft Word:

Ctrl + Enter: Adds a page break at the cursor location

Ctrl + Spacebar: Remove formatting from selected text

Home: Move cursor to beginning of current line

End: Move cursor to end of current line

Ctrl + Home: Move to the beginning of the **document**

Keyboard Plus Mouse

General:

Copy: Ctrl + Drag selected **file** to copy location

Create Shortcut: Ctrl + Shift + Drag selected file to shortcut location

Index and Vocabulary

Every piece of computer lingo I could find or think of to help you better understand.

Accelerators – See **Keyboard Accelerators**.

Address Bar – Located toward the top and usually centered or left aligned in your **browser**. This is where the **Internet Address** (or **URL**) for the current **web page** you are viewing is shown. Many **browsers** have a downward pointing arrow at the right side of this that you can click to see a short **history** of **sites** you have visited. If you know the **URL** of a site you want to visit you can enter it here. [pg. 33, 70, 71, 74, 75, 76, 79, 81, 95, 116]

Adware – Can be a type of **malware**. It is normally installed with other **software**, and is typically the cause of excessive pop-up adds.

'Always Connected' Internet – These days most sources of **Internet** don't require users to do anything special to get **online**. It is just there waiting whenever they want it. [pg. 93] Examples: **DSL**, Cable, Satellite

America Online – An **Internet** company normally related to searching, **e-mail**, and instant messaging.
Website: http://www.aol.com/

Anti-Malware – Some **browsers** have this built in to protect users from **viruses**, **worms**, **Trojans** and **spyware**. [pg. 95]

Anti-Phishing – Some **browsers** have this built in to protect users from **phishing** scams, by keeping a list of web forgery sites and warning you when you may be visiting a website that isn't legitimate. There is a group, APWG, dedicated to informing people about **phishing** at http://www.antiphishing.org

Anti-Virus – The **software** that keeps your computer safer from **viruses**, **Trojans** and other **malware**. It should always be running in the background. If it is working properly, you won't even notice it most of the time. This should be kept up to date as much as possible, but most **programs** have a setting to keep themselves up to date automatically as long as you are connected to the **Internet**. Many of these require paid subscriptions to keep you up to date, but some are free to use or to try. [pg. 94, 95]
Examples: **AVG Anti-Virus**, **Symantec AntiVirus**, **Norton AntiVirus**, **McAfee**.

Anti-Spyware – Similar to **anti-virus**, but not normally as dangerous to your computer. This doesn't need to be running all the time. It can just be updated and set to scan every once in a while. [pg. 94, 95]
Examples: **Ad-Aware** , **Spybot Search & Destroy** , **AVG Anti-Spyware**.

AOL – see **America Online**.

Apple – A large **software** and **hardware** corporation; creator of Macs, **Safari**, iPods, and others. Notice the capital letter 'A'. *Website*: http://www.apple.com/

Application – Synonym for **program**. [pg. 39, 65]

ASCII – Short for American Standard Code for Information Interchange. This is a standard format that computers use for saving **files** so that all of them can understand it.

Attachment – A **file** that is included in an **e-mail**. It is 'attached' to the **e-mail**. A paperclip is the typical symbol for attachments in **e-mails**. [pg. 84, 86, 87]

AVG Anti-Virus – **Anti-Virus** software written by AVG. There are basic free packages with limited protection and features including **anti-virus** protection. There are also larger more feature rich packages for sale. [pg. 94]
Website: http://free.avg.com/

Back Button – At the top left of every **browser** I've ever seen. It looks like an arrow pointing to the left. This takes you back to the previous **webpage** you were on before your most recent click on a **link**. [pg. 68, 74]
Shortcuts: Alt + left arrow key *or* Backspace key *or* Shift + mouse wheel down

Back slash (\) – Typically located above the Enter key on the **keyboard**, and used in paths inside your computer on Windows machines.

Bandwidth – Refers to the amount of data that can travel through a part of the **Internet**. More bandwidth typically means your **Internet** experience will be faster.

Blog – Short for Web Log. This is kind of like an **online** diary or soap box, and normally has a focused topic. Users typically post discussions and comments as well as allow responses about their topic.

Blue Screen of Death – When Windows operating systems **crash** beyond recovery the screen turns completely blue with a long descriptive message that isn't typically very helpful. From my experience most of these **crashes** are due to **driver** conflicts or failures and sometimes overheating of the computer.

Boot – Another way of saying "Turn on the Power to your computer." [pg. 11, 12]
Synonyms: Start, Startup

Browser – A **program** used for accessing information on the **Internet** by means of following **links** or searching through **webpages** on **websites**. The entire **link** of websites is known as the **World Wide Web**. [pg. 13, 14, 33, 38, 65, 68-71, 73-76, 79, 105-107, 116, 117]
Examples: **FireFox** , **Google Chrome** , **Internet Explorer** , **Opera** , and **Safari** .

Buffer – This is most commonly used when 'streaming' video or audio on the **Internet**. The video itself is continues to **download** while you begin watching before it finishes. The buffer is where the video is **downloaded** to while you begin watching or listening. This also helps slower **Internet** times become less noticeable.
Example: A buffer is like a line at a grocery store. People at the front of the line can start checking out even though the line isn't full (the part of the movie that is already **downloaded** can begin playing). At the same time the line continues to fill with other customers at the other end (the video continues **downloading** until you have all of it).

Bug – A mistake in a **program** or piece of **software**.

Burn – Copy **files** to a **CD** or **DVD**. You would 'burn' **files** to a CD if you wanted them copied onto the CD.

Cable Internet – **Internet** that comes through the same cable as a cable TV would. This is a form of '**always connected**' **Internet**. This form of **Internet** comes through a **cable modem**. Examples: Comcast, Cox, EarthLink.

Cable Modem – A **modem** that connects through your cable TV line. It allows your computer to connect to the **Internet** by using your **ISP**.

Cache – **Internet Browsers** keep some **website** information on your computer to help the site load faster the next time you visit. This is referred to as the cache. It's faster because the information is retrieved from your computer instead of the **Internet**. [pg. 14, 74]

Cancel Button – The 'X' that appears at the top right corner of most **applications** and **documents**. Clicking the button closes things down.

Cascading Style Sheet – See **CSS**.

Cat 5 Cable – Synonym for **Ethernet Cable**.

CD – See **Compact Disk**.

CD drive – A **device** used for reading and/or writing **CD**s. **CD-ROM drives**, **CD-R drives**, and **CD-RW drives** are all types of CD drives. [pg. 91]

CD-R – Short for CD Recordable. Must use a CD writable or **DVD** writable drive to record on these, but can read them with any CD or **DVD drive**. The data on these cannot be erased.

CD-R drive – A type of **CD drive** that can be used for reading **CD**s or writing to **CD-R**s.

CD-ROM drive – A type of **CD drive** used only for reading CDs. ROM stands for Read Only **Memory**.

CD-RW – Short for CD Recordable/Writable. Must use a CD writable or **DVD** writable drive to record on these, but can read them with any CD or **DVD drive**. The data on these can be erased and re-written with new data.

CD-RW drive – A type of **CD drive** that can be used for reading **CD**s, as well as writing **CD-R**s and **CD-RW**s.

Client – Your home computer is almost always a client, because it connects to **servers** on the **Internet** to get information for you. Client can also refer to the client side of **software** like **e-mail client** and **ftp client**.

Clip Art – Small picture **files** that come standard with editing **programs** like **Microsoft Word**. These pictures can be inserted into your **documents** to help clarify them or make them more interesting. [pg. 34]

Clipboard – This can be viewed as a small storage space where **files** or text are kept when they are **copied** or **cut** from somewhere in a **document** or on your computer. The basic clipboard only holds one item at a time, so you must **paste** before you copy or cut again. See chapter 4 for more on this. [pg. 30, 54, 56]

Compact Disk (CD) – A storage **device** made of plastic in the shape of a flat circle with a hole in the center of it. It spins in a **CD drive** and is read by a laser inside the drive.

Cookies – **Files** that are stored on your computer that **websites** use to remember things about you. If you use any kind of personalized website where you can change the settings, those settings are stored in a cookie on your computer. [pg. 74]

Crash – When your computer stops working normally due to **software** issues. [pg. 93] Synonyms: **froze**, died.

CRT Monitor – Stands for *Cathode Ray Tube*. These computer **monitors** are the typical old boxy looking ones. They are quickly being replaced by flat panel monitors as a standard.

CSS – These are **files** that are used on many websites to control the way the site looks. They can control colors, sizes, and positions of objects among other things. [pg. 105]

Database – Used for storing information in a logical manner to aid in quicker, more efficient future access.

Defrag – Short for **Defragment**.

Defragment – This is a method using **software** (normally the "defragmenter") to organize **files** on your **hard drive**. It doesn't move them within **folders** on your **hard drive**, it just organizes them on the actual physical **hard drive**. Your computer will not look any different after you defragment, but it may move ever so slightly faster. [pg. 16, 99, 100]

Desktop – In regards to computers, your desktop is what you're looking at when you have no **programs** or **documents** open. It is a sort of virtual desktop for you to start working from. If you have a background picture, it is on your desktop. [pg. 14, 21, 24, 25, 27, 29, 39, 40, 111-114, 116]

Devices – All of the **hardware** that attaches to the outside of your computer. [pg. 12, 43, 44] *Examples*: **Monitors, Printers, Speakers, Keyboard, Mouse, Digital Camera, Webcam**.

DHCP – Stands for *Dynamic Host Configuration Protocol*. This sort of setup just means that **IP addresses** are chosen for you automatically, so that you don't have to worry about what they are.

Dialog Box – Whenever **Windows** requires some information from you, it normally brings up a dialog box to collect this information. These boxes are just windows that don't usually appear in the taskbar, don't have a **minimize** button, and sometimes stay on top of all other windows.

Dial Up – A form of **Internet** that comes through your phone line. There is a phone number that you had to enter at one time to make the connection work. You must actually connect to the **Internet** every time you want to use it with this. This is typically slower than **Cable** or **DSL**, but it is cheaper. Your phone can not be used for calls while on the **Internet** in this manner. [pg. 89]
Examples: Juno, NetZero, PeoplePC Online.

Digital Camera – A camera that stores pictures and possibly video in some kind of digital format, normally .jpg that can be copied directly to your computer. [pg. 43, 44]

Digital Subscriber Line (DSL) – **Internet** that comes through a phone line, but doesn't stop you from using the phone. It is another form of **'Always Connected' Internet**. This form of **Internet** comes through a **DSL modem**.
Examples: Verizon, EarthLink, AT&T, Yahoo.

Directory – see **Folder**.

Directory Structure – This is how most computers are organized. It is a set of **folders**, and **folders** within **folders** for organizing **files** in a logical manner. Most computers these days are organized in what is called a tree structure, because there is a root **folder** which expands out into several **folders** that also expand into other **folders** like branches of a tree. In this organization your **files** are where the leaves of the tree would be.

DNS – Stands for *Domain Name Service*. All websites are actually stored at a location associated with an **IP address**, but IP addresses are hard to remember, so they are also associated with a name. The DNS **server** translates the name you type into the **IP address** so that you get to where you want to go.
Example: **Google** is located at 64.233.169.99, but all you have to type to get there is "www.google.com" (you can also type "google.com" which takes you to the same place).

Document – These normally have an **extension** of .doc, .pdf, .txt, or something similar. Most of the **files** on your computer that you open with other **programs** are documents. [pg. 12, 23, 29, 33, 34, 36-41, 46, 54-56, 58, 73, 84, 105, 117]
Examples: **HTML** document, Word document.

Download – The act of obtaining a **document** or **program** from a **website**. You download it to your computer. [pg. 12, 13, 34-36, 61-63, 65, 77, 84, 93-95, 97, 106, 107]

Drag and Drop – Action done with the **mouse** to move **files**. It involves clicking down on the left **mouse** button over the object, moving the object to where you want it, then releasing the **mouse** button.

Driver – The **software** that tells your computer how to talk to particular **hardware**. [pg. 43]

DSL – see **Digital Subscriber Line**.

Dual Core – Refers to a **processor** being able to streamline tasks by splitting information up and calculating two things at once. It must contain two 'cores' within the **processor** to accomplish this.

DVD – short for *Digital Video Disc*. These are a form of storage that look like **CD**s, but have quite a bit more space. They are normally used for videos because of the large **file** size involved.

DVD drive - A **device** used for reading and/or writing **DVD**s and **CD**s. **DVD-ROM drives**, **DVD-R drives**, and **DVD-RW drives** are all types of DVD drives. [pg. 91]

DVD-R – short for *DVD Recordable*. Must use a **DVD** writable drive to record on these, but can read them with any **DVD drive**. The data on these cannot be erased. A **CD** writable drive is not the same thing and cannot be used to record **DVD**s.

DVD-R drive - A type of **DVD drive** that can be used for reading **DVD**s and **CD**s or writing to **DVD-R**s and **CD-R**s.

DVD-ROM drive – A type of **DVD** drive used only for reading **DVD**s and **CD**s. ROM stands for Read Only **Memory**.

DVD-RW – short for *DVD Recordable/Writable*. Must use a **DVD** writable drive to record on these, but can read them with any **DVD drive**. The data on these can be erased and re-written with new data. A **DVD** writable drive is not the same thing and cannot be used to record **DVD**s.

DVD-RW drive - A type of **DVD drive** that can be used for reading **DVD**s and **CD**s, as well as writing **DVD-R**s, **DVD-RW**s, **CD-R**s and **CD-RW**s.

Electronic mail – see **e-mail**.

e-mail – Short for **electronic mail**. A way of sending written letters or **documents** to people over the **Internet**. You can think of it as a replacement for regular (postal) mail. [pg. 13, 14, 73, 75, 79, 81, 82, 84, 85, 87, 95, 96]
Examples: Gmail, Yahoo Mail, Hotmail, AOL mail, **Outlook Express**, **Thunderbird**.

e-mail client – You use an e-mail client to access an e-mail **server** to get your e-mails. An e-mail client is normally just referred to as your **e-mail**.

End User – In relation to **programs**, this is normally a reference to who will be using the **program**. You are the end user of the product.

Ethernet Adapter – Contains a port on your computer that looks similar to a phone jack, but slightly larger. Used for connecting to a **modem**, **router**, or **switch** through an **Ethernet cable**.

Ethernet Cable – This is the most common way to hook your computer up to your source of **Internet**. It typically connects your computer directly to your **router**.

Excel - A spreadsheet **program** written by **Microsoft** that has a lot of functions for creating tables of information and performing calculations. Open Office Calc can open Excel **files**. [pg. 34-36, 39, 47, 49, 61, 62, 107]

Executable – This can be used to **install** a **program**, or **launch** a **program** that is already installed. All of the **shortcuts** on your **desktop** or in the **start menu** are **links** to **executables** for **programs**. When you run a **program**, you either click on the executable or a **link** to the executable. [pg. 39, 41, 61-63, 84, 106]

eXtensible HyperText Markup Language (XHTML) – A type of **document** similar to **HTML file**s that can be opened by **browsers**. It contains aspects of HTML as well as **XML**.

eXtensible Markup Language (XML) – A type of organized **document** similar to **HTML file**s that can be opened by **browsers** and some other **document** viewers. It is exclusively a way to organize data and has nothing to do with how it is displayed.

Extension – Typically a group of three or four letters at the end of a **file** or **program** name following a dot(.) that signifies to the computer what kind of **file** it is. [pg. 105, 109]
Examples: .doc, .html, .jpg, .pdf, .txt

External Hard Drive – A **hard drive** that is outside of your computer typically inside of a plastic casing. It is usually connected to your computer using a **USB cable** or SATA cable. These can be used for extra storage or for transferring a large number of **files** between computers. [pg. 12, 16, 43, 45]

FAQ – Stands for *Frequently Asked Questions*.

FireFox – An **Internet Browser** designed by the **Mozilla Foundation**. It is free to **download** and use. [pg. 13, 14, 39, 50, 65-69, 72-75, 105-107]

File – Your computer is composed of lots of **files** and **folders**. **Documents** and **executables** are types of **files**. [pg. 12, 15, 16, 20-27, 32, 33, 35, 37-41, 43, 47, 54-59, 61-63, 65, 73, 74, 76 77, 84-86, 97, 99, 105-107, 109, 112, 116, 117]
Examples: Word **documents**, **Excel** workbooks, pictures, songs, and videos.

File Transfer Protocol (FTP) – The **protocol** designed for transferring all kinds of **files** on the **Internet**. Usually used for **uploading file**s to a **server** on the **Internet**, or **downloading file**s to your computer from a **server**.

Firewall – A **program** on your computer that blocks most unwanted people and **programs** from accessing your computer from the **Internet**. [pg. 93]

Flash Drive – A small **device** that is used to store information like pictures or **documents**. **Digital cameras** contain some form of flash drive or **memory stick** (there are several styles). **USB** flash drives can be plugged directly into your computer and are typically used for transferring **files** between computers. [pg. 16, 44]
Synonyms: Memory Stick, Thumb Drive

Folder – A container for **files** and other folders, in the same way that real folder holds papers. It is used to group **files** that have something in common, and keep your computer organized. A folder is also known as a **directory**. [pg. 12, 24-27, 33, 37-41, 54-59, 72, 77, 96, 97, 105]

Formatter – A **program** capable of changing the internal format of a **document**. [pg. 34]
Example: Microsoft Word is a word **document** formatter.

Forward Button – Located at the top left of **browsers**, always just to the right of the **back button**. This button works as an undo for the **back button**. If you press the **back button** followed immediately by the forward button you will end up on the page you started with.
Shortcuts: Alt + left arrow key *or* Shift + mouse wheel up

Forward slash (/) – Typically located to the left of one of the Shift keys and sharing a key with the question mark('?') on the **keyboard**, and used in paths for website addresses and on **Linux** machines.

Froze – When your computer stops responding to commands or input, you can say it froze. [pg. 24] *Synonyms*: hung, stopped responding.

FTP – see **File Transfer Protocol**.

FTP Client – A **program** used to connect to an **ftp server** by giving a **username** and **password**. If you need to **upload file**s to the **Internet**, this is the **software** you would use to do it. It can also be used for **downloading**.
Examples: WinSCP , SSH Secure File Transfer Client , WS_FTP.

FTP Server – This is where you **upload** a **file** to when you want to put it on the **Internet**. A **file** that you want to **download** had to be **uploaded** to a **server** at some point. Many times it is done to an FTP server using an **FTP Client**.

GB – See **Gigabyte**.

Gigabyte (GB) – A measure of the units of storage on your computer. A Gigabyte is about 1,000 **Megabytes (MB)**; actually closer to 1,024 **MB**. **Memory** and **Hard drive** space are typically measured in Gigabytes these days. For comparison a writable CD typically holds about 700 **MB**, while a writable **DVD** typically holds several GB. [pg. 15 - 17, 44]

GIMP - Stands for GNU Image Manipulation Program. Used for viewing and editing pictures and other images. Comes with some **Linux** systems, but can also be **downloaded** for free at the gimp website.
Website: http://www.gimp.org/

Google – See **Google Search Engine**.

Google Chrome 🌀 – an **Internet Browser** designed by **Google**. It can be **downloaded** for free. [pg. 13, 65, 67, 68, 71-75]
Website: http://www.google.com/chrome

Google Search Engine – Most often referred to as **Google**, although **Google** is also the name of the company that created it. This is a website used for searching for almost anything on the World Wide Web. [pg. 9, 35, 61]
Website: http://www.google.com

Graphics Card – The piece of **hardware** that sends information for display to your **monitor**. The **monitor** cable is always connected to the graphics card. Sometimes the graphics card is a separate piece of hardware plugged into the inside of your computer, and sometimes it is integrated with your **motherboard**.
Synonyms: Video Card, Video Adapter

GUI – Stands for *Graphical User Interface*. Almost every **program** you use these days has a GUI, which just means that you can use a **mouse** to move around and click buttons and options that you want.

Hard disk – A synonym for **hard drive**.

Hard drive – The physical location where all of the **files** on your computer are stored. Anytime you save a **document** it is put on your hard drive so that it can be accessed later. The hard drive keeps information stored even when the computer is turned off. [pg. 12, 15-18, 37, 40, 41, 44, 45, 97, 99, 100]

Hardware – The physical computer and all of the physical things that can attach to it or are contained within it. [pg. 14, 15, 17, 89, 90, 97]
Examples: The actual computer, **hard drive**, **monitor**, and other **devices**.

HD – stands for **High Definition**.

History – **Internet Browsers** keep track of **sites** that are visited to aid in quicker use the next time, as well as to help users so they don't have to remember where they've been. The history is used for the **forward** and **back buttons** among other things.

Homepage – Used in two ways. First, **websites** have homepages. When you enter a website, this is like going in the front door. This the page that is supposed to be set up in a manner that gives you a good idea of what information the **site** contains without having to look through all of it yourself. Second, your **browser** also has a homepage which is the **webpage** that opens automatically when you **launch** the **browser**. [pg. 14, 68-70, 77, 117]

Hover – Action with the **mouse** that involves allowing the **mouse** pointer to sit in one spot over an object on the screen. This is normally a way of bringing up tooltips or other hidden information. **Links** on websites may also change color or style when you hover over them with the **mouse**.

HTML – see **HyperText Markup Language**.

HTTP – see **HyperText Transfer Protocol**.

HTTPS – see **HyperText Transfer Protocol Secure**.

Hyperlink – More often referred to as **links**. They are the virtual connections between different **web pages** on the **Internet**. These are what you click on to move from one web page to the next.

HyperText Markup Language (**HTML**) - One of the languages that a **browser** can understand. It tells the **browser** where to place the text and pictures on the **website**.

HyperText Transfer Protocol (**HTTP**) – The **protocol** designed for organizing how **webpages** are moved from **servers** to **browsers**. Most **URL**s for normal **web sites** begin with: http:// [pg. 76]

HyperText Transfer Protocol Secure (**HTTPS**) – An extension of **HTTP** that is designed to be secure. **URL**s for these sites will begin with https:// and will normally be slightly slower than sites that just use **HTTP**, but will be much more secure.

Icon – Small pictures seen on your **desktop** and in **folders** on your computer that designate **files** and **programs**. The look of the icon is determined by the **extension** of the **file** or the type of **program**. [pg. 14, 15, 21, 29, 38-41, 69, 71, 90, 93]
  Examples: A **Word document** looks like a lined piece of paper with a 'w' in the top left corner, An **Excel** spreadsheet looks like a couple of cells from a **spreadsheet** with an 'x' in the top left corner.

IE – see **Internet Explorer**.

IM – see **Instant Messenger**.

Install – The process you go through in order to make a **program** work on your computer. Most **programs** come with several **files** that work together to do what you want them to do. You don't need to know about these, so the installer puts them where they need to go so that the **program** will work. The installer normally includes and **executable** to initiate the install. [pg. 63, 65, 66, 93, 105, 106]

Instant Messenger (IM) – A **program** used for chatting with people in real time on the **Internet**. *Examples*: AOL Instant messenger, Google Talk 🔲, Windows Messenger 🔲, Yahoo Messenger 🔲, Meebo, Skype.

Internet – A massive connection of computers of all different varieties using wires, satellites, and wireless signals. These computers are normally separated into two categories: **clients** and **servers**. When you are looking at a **website**, **downloading** a **file**, or using an **instant messenger**, you are connected to the Internet. You can think of the Internet as a **network** of **networks**. [pg. 13, 14, 44, 52, 65, 70, 71, 76, 79, 80, 87, 89, 90, 93, 94]

Internet Address – This is what you see in the **address bar** of your **browser**. It is more commonly referred to as a **URL**. The first couple of letters are normally **http**, **https**, or ftp.
   Examples:
      http://www.google.com/
      http://www.aol.com/
      http://www.msn.com/
      http://www.apple.com/
      http://www.yahoo.com/

Internet Browser – See **Browser**.

Internet Explorer (IE) 🔲 – An **Internet Browser** designed by **Microsoft**. This comes pre-installed on all **Windows** machines. It can also be **downloaded** for free. [pg. 9, 13, 14, 50, 65-75, 105-107, 116]

Internet Service Provider (ISP) – This is the company that allows you to get to the **Internet** using your computer, most often for a fee. **Internet** can come through **Dial Up**, **DSL**, **Cable**, or **Satellite Dish**. Examples: Comcast, Quest, Dish Network, AOL, EarthLink, Juno.

IP Address – If your computer is connected to the **Internet**, it is assigned an IP address to uniquely identify it. IP addresses are a series of 4 numbers between 0 and 255 separated by dots. These numbers have specific meanings, but you shouldn't have to worry about them, as long as you have an IP address you can probably access the **Internet**. Your computer is typically automatically assigned an IP address by your **router**.
   Examples:
      192.168.0.1
      10.10.10.75
      255.255.255.255

ISP – see **Internet Service Provider**.

iTunes - A music player written by **Apple**. It can be used to organize and share music libraries as well. [pg. 106, 107]

Kate - Text editor and **formatter** on **Linux** systems; similar to **WordPad** on **Windows**, but with some other useful functionality. [pg. 22, 34]

KB – See **Kilobyte**.

KEdit - Text editor on **Linux** systems; very similar to **Notepad** on **Windows**. [pg. 33]

Keyboard – The tool you use to type with and send other commands to your computer. [pg. 11, 12, 29, 30, 32, 33, 36, 43, 44, 69, 102, 116]

Keyboard Accelerators – These are keystrokes, or a series of keystrokes on the **keyboard** that help you accomplish tasks without using the **mouse**. [pg. 10]

Keylogger – **Spyware** that records what is typed on your computer. It can be used to obtain information about you like account numbers, user names, and **passwords**.

Keystroke Logging – This is what a **keylogger** does; act of recording keystrokes on a computer.

Kilobyte (**KB**) – A measure of the units of storage on your computer. A Kilobyte is about 1,000 bytes; actually closer to 1,024 bytes. Bytes are the basic units for storage on your computer.

Konquer - an **Internet Browser** on some **Linux** systems. It can be **downloaded** for free.

Konqueror – an **Internet Browser** on some **Linux** systems. It can be **downloaded** for free.

KView - Picture viewer on **Linux** systems; very similar to **Windows Picture and Fax Viewer** on **Windows**.

KWrite - Text editor and **formatter** on **Linux** systems; very similar to **WordPad** on **Windows**. [pg. 34]

LAN – Stands for *Local Area Network*. By connecting computers together you are creating a LAN. The **network** inside of your house is normally referred to as a LAN; it is the small grouping of two or more computers you have typically connected to a single **router**.

Landscape (horizontal) – Orientation for printing where the paper has its long way running from left to right. [pg. 47-52]

Launch – Typically done by clicking on an **executable**, or a **shortcut** to an **executable** to open a **program**. Synonyms: start, execute, run. [pg. 106]

Link – These are normally highlighted words or pictures on web pages that allow you to go to another page or **download** something by clicking on them. [pg. 39-41, 61, 70, 73, 79-82, 85, 86, 95, 117]

Linux – Any of a group of **Operating Systems** that are created by groups of individuals on the **Internet**, as opposed to a company like **Microsoft** or **Apple**. They are referred to as open source because the code used to write them is available for anyone to see. Examples: Red Hat, **Ubuntu**. [pg. 11, 18, 33-35, 54, 95]

LCD Monitor – Stands for *Liquid-Crystal Display*. This is a type of computer **monitor**. It is used in most laptops, and in flat panel **monitors** for desktops as well as some **HD** TVs. They consume less power than **CRT Monitors**, as well as take up less space and produce better, sharper images.

Login – This is what you do with secure **programs** or **websites** using your personal **username** and **password** to access parts of the **program** or website that you couldn't otherwise, or to personalize certain aspects. Some computer setups also require you to log in with a **username** and **password**. It is a way of getting permission to do things that you couldn't otherwise. [pg. 113]
Synonyms: Logon, Log In, Log On

Logoff – The opposite of **Login**. This is a way of telling the computer that you are done with those services that are associated with the **login**.

Logon – See **Login**.

Logout – See **Logoff**.

Mac – Short for **Macintosh**. [pg. 14, 31]

Mac Book – A laptop computer made by **Apple**. [pg. 11]

Macintosh – Most often shortened to **Mac** these days. The line of personal computers made by **Apple**.

Mac OS – **Operating system** written by **Apple**. It comes with most **Mac** computers, like the MacBook. [pg. 11, 14]

Malware – An all encompassing word for bad things like: **viruses**, **worms**, **Trojans** and **spyware**. Any **programs** that fall into this category are meant to cause harm to your computer, or steal your information, or another user's information. Malware is a shorthand version of *malicious software*. [pg. 95]

Maximize ▢ ▢ ▢ ▢ – Button in the top right corner of most **programs** and **folders** that looks like a single rectangle sometimes with a thicker top border. This makes the **program** take up the whole screen. [pg. 18-20, 22, 23, 116]

MB – See **Megabyte**. [pg. 16, 84]

McAfee – Computer security company. They have McAfee **virus** protection **software**. *Website*: http://www.mcafee.com [pg. 94]

Megabits – A unit of measure for **network** speeds.

Megabyte (**MB**) – A measure of the units of storage on your computer. A Megabyte is about 1,000 **Kilobytes** (**KB**); actually closer to 1,024 **KB**. Some **Memory** is still measured in Megabytes these days, but is becoming less common since we are moving up to **Gigabytes**.

Memory – Also referred to as **RAM**. This is where **programs** and **documents** are temporarily stored while you are using them, allowing faster access. These days memory is typically measured in **GigaBytes** (GB). The memory is typically one of the easiest things to upgrade on a computer, because the computer contains snap in slots that can be replaced when the computer is off.

Memory Stick – A small **device** that is used to store information like pictures or **documents**. **Digital cameras** contain some form of memory stick (there are several styles). **USB** memory sticks can be plugged directly into your computer and are typically used for transferring **files** between computers. [pg. 43-45]
Synonyms: **Flash Drive**, Thumb Drive

Menu – A list of items that can be clicked. [pg. 83]

Microsoft – A large **software** corporation; creator of **Windows**, **Internet Explorer** and **Microsoft Office**. [pg. 11, 61-63]

Microsoft Internet Explorer – More commonly referred to as **Internet Explorer**.

Microsoft Office – The entire group of **programs** that are typically distributed together by **Microsoft** including **Excel**, **PowerPoint** and **Word**. [pg. 34-36, 61]

Microsoft Office Excel – See **Excel**.

Microsoft Office Picture Manager –See **Picture Manager**.

Microsoft Office PowerPoint – See **PowerPoint**.

Microsoft Office Word – See **Word**.

Minimize – Button in the top right corner of most **programs** and **folders** that looks like a small horizontal line. This moves the **program** out of the way and down to the toolbar at the bottom of the screen. [pg. 18-23, 116]

Modem – The **device** that connects you to the **Internet** through an **Internet Service Provider (ISP)**. This should be the first thing that is connected to the wire that comes out of the wall for your **Internet**. Side Note: The word modem comes from a combination of the words "modulate" and "demodulate" because that was what it originally did with computer signals to phone lines. [pg. 89]

Monitor – Looks similar to a TV, this is where all the information from your computer is displayed; also known as a screen. [pg. 11, 12, 43, 44, 90]

Mouse – The **device** you use with your computer in order to move your pointer or cursor around the screen. It has a one-to-one mapping with the screen, which just means that if you move it forward on the table (away from you) the cursor move up on the screen, and if you move the mouse toward you the cursor moves down on the screen. [pg. 10-12, 36, 38, 40, 41, 43, 44, 54, 58, 59, 75, 81, 100, 101, 116, 117]

Mozilla Firefox – See **Firefox**.

Mozilla Foundation – **Firefox** and **Thunderbird** are products of Mozilla. They are groups of people who contribute to the project and distribute the **software** for free.

Netscape Navigator – **Internet Browser** written by Netscape Communications Corporation which is also a contributor to **Mozilla**. Owned by **AOL** and officially discontinued on December 28, 2007. If you're still using this you should probably **download** a new **browser**.

Network – A group of two or more computers connected so that they can talk to each other. You can set up a home network in your house so that the computers there can see and share **files** with one another. [pg. 46, 47, 89, 90]

Network Adapter – see **Network Interface Card**.

Network Card – see **Network Interface Card**.

Network Interface Card (NIC) – The **hardware** that allows your computer to connect to a **network** using a network cable (**Ethernet cable**).
Synonyms: Network Adapter, Network Card, NIC

NIC – see **Network Interface Card**.

Norton - **Anti-virus** software written by **Symantec**. [pg. 94]
Website: http://www.symantec.com/

Notepad – A simple text editor that is included with all versions of **Microsoft** Windows. It is typically found under Start -> Programs -> Accessories. [pg. 21, 22, 33, 54, 57, 58, 105, 107]

Num Lock – stands for Number Lock. It's a key on the **keyboard** normally at the top left of the **Num Pad**. [pg. 32]

Num Pad – The small grouping of keys typically on the right side of the **keyboard**. It contains things like numbers, plus(+), minus(-) and Enter.

Offline Files – Sometimes your **browser** keeps entire copies of **web pages** to aid in faster loading in the future. [pg. 74]

Online – Normally refers to being connected to the **Internet**, but can also refer to when you sign into an **Instant Messenger** or other **program**. [pg. 9, 13, 31, 35, 65, 94, 96]

OpenOffice – A free office environment with word processing, **spreadsheet**, and presentation tools. [pg. 34-36, 61]
Website: http://www.openoffice.org

OpenOffice Calc – The OpenOffice spreadsheet tool for creating lists and performing calculations on data. [pg. 35, 61, 107]

OpenOffice Writer – The OpenOffice word processor for creating and modifying letters, papers, and other **documents**. [pg. 34, 61, 105-107]

Opera – A **browser** initially written by Telenor, a telecom company in Norway, now run by Opera Software ASA. There is a free version that can be **downloaded** online. [pg. 13, 14, 51, 65, 67-69, 71-75, 105-107]

Operating System – The **software** that helps your computer **software** talk to your computer **hardware**. You can't do much with a computer if it doesn't have an operating system on it. Examples: Windows XP, Windows Vista, Windows 7, Mac OS X, **Red Hat Linux**, **Ubuntu**. [pg. 9, 11, 12, 14-16, 22, 63, 93]

OS – Short for **Operating System**.

Outlook Express – An **e-mail client** distributed by **Microsoft** that resides on your computer. Allows you to **download** your **e-mail** so that you can view it while not connected to the Internet. [pg. 79, 81]

Paint - Picture editing **program** that comes standard on every copy of **Windows**. [pg. 35, 105-107]

Password – The set of letters, numbers and characters that are used in combination with a **username** to log into computers or websites. They should be hard to guess and kept secret. [pg. 75, 77]

Picture Manager - Picture and Image editor and organizer that comes with some copies of **Microsoft Office**. [pg. 35, 36, 105-107]

PC – Stands for *Personal Computer*. [pg. 11, 14]

PDF – This is the **extension** that appears on **files** that can be opened in adobe reader. It is short for Portable **Document** Format, because it is meant to be a form that can be opened on any computer with any **operating system**. [pg. 34, 63, 65, 66, 84, 106]

Phisher – People who engage in the act of **phishing**. [pg. 81]

Phishing – A method of scamming information from people by convincing them you are someone you're not, or any other way of fraudulently obtaining sensitive information from people. One common method is to put a **link** in an **e-mail** that takes you to their website, which they have set up to look exactly like another site you use, perhaps your bank. This is why it is important to look at the **URL**s of **links** that you follow to important web pages. [pg. 95]

Portrait (vertical) – Orientation for printing where the paper has its long way running from top to bottom. [pg. 47] Portrait

PowerPoint - A presentation creation tool made by **Microsoft** that allows you to build your own slideshows and presentations. PowerPoint **files** can be opened by OpenOffice Impress . [pg. 36, 48, 49, 61, 62, 106]

Plugin - Little pieces of **software** that can be added to your **browser** to give it more functionality, to make it nice, or generally just to make it better. They are called plugins because they are "plugged in" to your **browser** to make it better. They are generally free to **download**. [pg. 65, 66]

Printer – The physical **device** used for putting your **documents** in paper form. [pg 43-47]

Processor – This is the brain of your computer. It decides how to run everything. It's speed is normally measured in Gigahertz (GHz). They can also be **dual core** or **quad core**. [pg. 15, 17, 18]
Examples: Intel, AMD, Celeron.

Program – This is the **executable** you click on to make something happen on your computer. It is the environment you work in when trying to accomplish specific tasks. [pg. 11, 15, 16, 18-24, 29, 31, 33, 39, 40, 47, 61, 77, 79, 81, 84, 93-95, 97, 100, 105]
Examples: Internet Explorer, **Microsoft Word**, and **iTunes**.

Protocol – A set of specific steps that are followed by computer **programs** for communicating with each other.

Quad Core – Refers to a **processor** being able to streamline tasks by splitting information up and calculating up to four things at once. It must contain four 'cores' within the **processor** to accomplish this.

QuickTime - A music and video player written by **Apple**. [pg. 35, 65, 66, 105, 107]

QuickTime Picture Viewer - Picture viewing **program** that comes with **QuickTime**. [pg. 35, 105, 107]

RAM – see **Memory**. Stands for Random Access Memory.

RealPlayer – A music and video player. [pg. 65, 106, 107]

Reboot – Another way of saying "Restart your computer". [pg. 89, 90, 98]

Red Hat Linux – A **Linux** based **operating system** distributed by Red Hat. Website: www.redhat.com

Registry – see **Windows Registry**.

Resolution – Is a way of telling you how many pixels can fit on your screen. For example, if your resolution were 1280 x 1024, it would mean that you have 1,280 pixels across, and 1,024 pixels from top to bottom. **Monitors** typically have a standard resolution that they look best at. The larger the numbers, the more stuff that can be displayed on your screen, but the smaller all of it will look.
Examples: 1024 x 768

Restore – When a **program** has been **minimized**, it shows up in the taskbar, which is normally located at the bottom of the screen. Clicking on this is one way to restore the **program** to be displayed on the screen again. [pg. 17-23, 116]

Rip – Copy **files** (normally music) from a **CD** to your computer.

RJ-45 cable – Synonym for **Ethernet Cable**.

Router – **Device** used to assign **IP addresses** to computers on your **network**. This is normally connected to your **modem**, then to your computers to help them access the **Internet**. [pg. 89]

Roxio – A type of CD recording **software**.

Safari 🖥 – A **browser** written by **Apple** and distributed with **Mac** computers. Also free to **download**. [pg. 13, 14, 52, 65, 67-69, 72-75, 105-107]

Scanner – A **device** used for making digital copies of your paper **documents**.

Search Box – Most **browsers** have this at the top to the right of the **address bar**. It uses the **search engine** for you without having to go to the search engine's **web page** to do so. Most web sites these days also have a search box somewhere on their home page that lets you search within their site. These boxes are where you enter text describing what you are looking for.

Search Engine – This is what you use to find what you're looking for on the **Internet**. This can be in the form of its own webpage like **Google**, Yahoo, AOL and MSN, which all have a box where you can type in words to search for. It can also be part of the **browser** itself normally up at the top right, and sometimes the top left of your **browser**. [pg. 65]

Search Field – see **Search Box**.

Server – These are the machines on the **Internet** that keep everything running. They all have tasks that they are responsible for. When you request information on the **Internet** in any form, a server is the machine that gives it to you. Examples: **e-mail** servers, web servers, ftp servers. [pg. 76, 77]

Service Pack – In the **Windows operating system**, these are large important updates that help keep your computer secure and working properly. [pg. 15, 17]

Shortcut – These are **links** to other items on your computer. They help you organize things so that you don't remember where everything is located on your **hard drive**. Most of the **icons** on your **Desktop** are shortcuts to **executables** for **programs**. [pg. 22, 23, 29, 39, 69, 71, 116]

Site – see **Website**.

Software – In reference to computers, this word can most often be interchanged with **program**, but normally software is a broader term. If someone asked you what software you have on your computer, you would be correct in listing some of the **programs** you have installed. [pg. 13, 14, 33, 43, 44, 61, 63, 65, 89, 94, 97]

Soundcard – The piece of **hardware** that sends sound information to your **speakers** or headphones. It also typically has a plug for microphone input.

Spam – Another name for junk mail in your **e-mail** inbox. [pg. 83, 96]

Speakers – The physical **devices** used to produce sound created by your computer. [pg. 43]

Spreadsheet – A **document** with rows and columns where data can be entered and manipulated. **Excel** can be used for making spreadsheets. [pg. 34, 84]

Spyware – Malicious **software** that people use to gather information about you in order to **spam** you with products or steal other more important information. Unlike **viruses**, **spyware** doesn't typically spread itself to other computers.
Examples: **Keyloggers**

Start Menu – This normally resides in the lower left-hand corner of your screen, but it can be moved. It also typically has the word 'start' written on it. This is a menu bar that can be used for accessing everything on your computer. [pg. 14, 33-35, 40, 45, 97, 113]

Switch – Helps connect several **devices** together using **Ethernet cables**.

Symantec – **Internet** security company responsible for **Norton** AntiVirus among others. [pg. 94]
Website: http://www.symantec.com

Tabbed Browsing – Viewing several **webpages** at one time in the same **browser** window. They appear as 'tabs' along the top of the **browser** window. [pg. 69, 70]

TB – See **Terabyte**.

TCP/IP – The **protocol** (language/set of rules) used by computers to talk to each other on the **Internet**. Stands for Transmission Control Protocol/Internet Protocol.

Terabyte (TB) – A measure of the units of storage on your computer. A Terabyte is about 1,000 **Gigabytes** (GB); actually closer to 1,024 GB. Newer **hard drives** are starting to have storage in the range of Terabytes.

Title Bar – The long rectangular bar at the very top of any **program** or window, which gives you information about the program or window you have open. Example: If you have Microsoft Word open, the title bar tells you the name of the **document** you're working on and states that this is Microsoft **Word** you're looking at among other things. [pg. 19, 38]

Thunderbird – An **e-mail client** that can be installed on your computer. Comes with some **Linux** distributions. [pg. 81]

Trojan – Malicious **software** that is disguised as something else. It can cause anything from destruction of **files**, collecting data from your computer, to allowing someone else access to your computer when they shouldn't have it. The name 'Trojan' is short for 'Trojan Horse' borrowed from Homer's Iliad.

Ubuntu – A **Linux** based **Operating System** maintained and distributed as part of the Ubuntu project, which is community maintained (not a commercial company). [pg. 11] Website: www.ubuntulinux.com

Upload – This is the opposite of **download**. Uploading normally requires some sort of **ftp server** where you are required to **login** with a user name and **password**. [pg. 85]

Uniform Resource Locator (URL) – see **Internet Address**.

Unix – **Linux** operating systems are based on Unix.

URL – Stands for **Uniform Resource Locator**. See **Internet Address**. [pg. 71, 77, 116]

USB – Short for Universal Serial Bus, this is one of the ways that cables for **hardware** can be connected to your computer. [pg. 43-45, 52]

USB port – The slot on your computer where USB **devices** can be plugged in.

Username – A unique name that you had to register for your computer or a website for use of logging in. It is usually used in combination with a **password**. [pg. 77, 85, 96, 113]

Video Adapter – see **Video Card**.

Video Card – see **Graphics Card**.

Virus – Malicious **software** normally with the intention of spreading itself to other computers in order to cause more harm. **Anti-Virus** software can help keep **viruses** off of your computer.

WAN – Stands for *Wide Area Network*.

Web Address – see **Internet Address**.

Web Browser – see **Browser**.

Webcam – Short for **Web Camera**.

Web Camera – A **device** used for getting video and pictures directly to your computer. These are sometimes used for things like video conferences or video chats on the **Internet**.

Webpage – A collection of text and/or graphics for displaying information from a **document**. **HTML** is what they are written in so that your **browser** can read them. Example: In the **URL** http://www.3e-web.com/index.html the name if the webpage is *index.html*.

Website – Sometimes referred to as **site**. The **Internet** is a very large connection of websites. This is a grouping of **web pages** that typically have a common theme or topic.
        Examples: amazon.com

WiFi – Normally used as a synonym for 'Wireless **Internet**.'

Wiki – A website that allows anyone to add or modify content. They typically have moderators to prevent **spam** or other vandalism when changes are made.

Windows – **Operating System** distributed by **Microsoft**. There are quite a few versions of Windows operating systems including **Windows 2000**, **Windows XP**, and **Windows Vista**.

Windows 2000 – **Operating System** distributed by **Microsoft**.

Windows Media Player – A music and video player written by **Microsoft**.

Windows ME - **Operating System** distributed by **Microsoft**.

Windows Picture and Fax Viewer - .

Windows Registry – A **database** that Windows uses to store settings about itself and **programs** that are installed. Modifying the **registry** is best left to computer experts, because messing something up in the **registry** can cause your computer to malfunction.

Windows Vista - **Operating System** distributed by **Microsoft**.

Windows XP - **Operating System** distributed by **Microsoft**.

Word - A word processing **program** written by **Microsoft** that has a lot of power for creating **documents** and composing papers. Word **files** can be opened by **OpenOffice Writer** . [pg. 32-34, 39, 48, 49, 61, 63, 105, 117]

Word Processor – Used for composing or editing text based **documents**.

Worksheet – The writable area on a **spreadsheet** like **Excel**.

World Wide Web (www) – Located on the **Internet**, this is the group of all **web pages** and **web sites**. Pages are typically written in **HTML**, **XHTML**, **XML**, or other similar languages and interpreted by **browsers**. This is where you will spend most, if not all of your time on the **Internet**. See Chapter 5 for more information.
Synonyms: The Web

Worm – Malicious **software** that copies itself all over a **network** which eats up **bandwidth** and slows things down.

Writable CD – see **CD-RW**.

www – See **World Wide Web**.

XHTML – see **eXtensible HyperText Markup Language**.

XML – see **eXtensible Markup Language**.

Bibliography

There are no sources in the current document.

Excel 2007: The Missing Manual by Matthew MacDonald, 978-0-596-52759-4

The Complete Idiot's Guide to the Internet Second Edition by Peter Kent, 1-56761-535-X

The Design of Everyday Things by Donald A. Norman, 0-465-06710-7

Windows XP All-in-One Desk Reference for Dummies by Woody Leonhard, 0-7645-1548-9

Windows XP Home Edition: The Missing Manual by David Pogue, 0-596-00897-X

Computer Hope.com http://www.computerhope.com/

Media College.com http://www.mediacollege.com/internet/

W3Schools Online Web Tutorials http://www.w3schools.com/

OpenOffice.org http://www.openoffice.org/

WorldStart.com http://www.worldstart.com

DomainPurpose.com http://www.domainpurpose.com/tldext.htm

Webopedia http://www.webopedia.com/quick_ref/

Lavasoft http://www.lavasoft.com/

Spybot Search & Destroy http://www.safer-networking.org/en/spybotsd/

McAfee http://www.mcafee.com/us/

Symantec http://www.symantec.com/norton/index.jsp

AVG http://free.avg.com/us-en/

www.ingramcontent.com/pod-product-compliance
Lightning Source LLC
Chambersburg PA
CBHW041418050326
40689CB00002B/556